GREEN SIDE UP

Straight talk on growing and operating a profitable landscaping business!

By Ed Laflamme

EDITOR: Cindy Code
ART DIRECTOR: Mark Rook
DESIGN & LAYOUT: Samantha Gilbride
PRODUCTION DIRECTOR: Helen Duerr
COVER ILLUSTRATION: Peter Siu

Address all correspondence to:
GIE Media, Inc.
4020 Kinross Lakes Pkwy.
Richfield, Ohio 44286
800-456-0707

Library of Congress Control Number: 2007931311
ISBN: 978-1-883751-19-7

DEDICATION

To my Mom,
boy do I wish she could
have seen my book.
My wife Oriana
and our two boys,
Theo and Alex,
the sunshine in our lives.

TABLE OF CONTENTS

Acknowledgements   9

About the Author   11

Foreword   13

Introduction   15

Part One: Your Business   17

Part Two: Your Money   45

Part Three: Your People   87

Part Four: Your Operations   125

Part Five: Acquiring Your Customers   165

Part Six: Retaining Your Customers   211

Part Seven: You   239

Conclusion   263

Resources   265

Recommended Reading   267

ACKNOWLEDGEMENTS

Writing this book, my first, has been both excruciatingly painful and wildly exhilarating. At its completion I have a profoundly greater respect for authors the world over, and a new appreciation for the quality of patience.

With that said I need to first thank my wife, Oriana, for her love, encouragement and understanding while I worked on my book in "my cave." Her support was so appreciated especially in those "excruciatingly painful" times.

I owe a debt of gratitude to my West Coast buddy, Bill Arman. Bill listened, inspired and helped me organize my thoughts as the book progressed. He gave me the idea for the title as were were talking on our cell phones; I was driving on one of Connecticut's highways and he was driving on a California freeway. Yikes! That's life in the fast lane.

My friend, Judy Guido, an expert in sales and marketing, reviewed these sections for me, and thankfully mentioned I was missing a critical chapter. Great catch Jude, thanks.

A big thanks goes to Joe Castignoli, the vice president of finance of my former company, who reviewed, edited and then blessed the financial parts of the book.

Mark Stevens, my friend, mentor and author of more than 20 books including two best sellers, *Your Marketing Sucks* and *Your Management Sucks*. I want to thank you for encouragement, advice and inspiration.

I owe thanks to fellow consultant and friend, Ellen Ely of Training Solutions, for her input in the people section.

And, Debbie Fay of Bespeak Presentation Solutions of Fairfield, CT, a huge thanks for her work on the editing and organization of the book. Thank you so much Debbie.

Lastly, I thank all of the people currently or previously associated with *Lawn & Landscape* magazine especially Jeff Fenner who liked the concept for the book, started the ball rolling and introduced me to Steve Smith, former books editor. I also need to acknowl-edge Roger Stanley, former editor of *Lawn & Landscape* for his help in editing and encour-agement as the book progressed. A special thanks goes to Cindy Code, Editorial Director for *Lawn & Landscape* and *Golf Course Industry*, for bringing all the forces of the magazine together, and for the long hours spent editing and corresponding as the book was com-pleted. Thanks so much, Cindy, for "bringing the book around the bases and finally to home plate." I hope readers enjoy the fruits of the efforts of so many great people, and that it helps all the landscaper contractors who read it. Now let's go and make it happen!

October 2007

Ed Laflamme

Grass Roots Consulting

ABOUT THE AUTHOR

Ed Laflamme

Ed Laflamme has been knee deep in landscaping since 1971, and is a nationally recognized and respected leader in the green industry today. With $700 borrowed from his mother, Ed bought two mowers and began his landscaping business servicing clients out of the trunk of his car. Nine years later he sold the residential segment of his business and concentrated his energies on the commercial and industrial sectors. He set his sites on the mother of all commercial contracts: General Electric's World Headquarters, located in Fairfield, Conn. In 1985 he was awarded their business; his first multi-million dollar account. With GE on his customer list Laflamme was unstoppable. Over the next 10 years he acquired maintenance contracts for Xerox, ABB, Olin Chemical, GE Capital, Travelers Insurance, Bristol Meyers, GTE, GenRE, Philips Medical and many more. By this time, company sales had reached more than $5 million, making Laflamme Services, Inc., the largest landscape maintenance contractor in Connecticut. In 1998, Laflamme Services, Inc. was listed as one of the top 100 revenue-generating landscape companies in America by *Lawn & Landscape* magazine. In 1999, Laflamme sold his company to Landcare USA. At the time Laflamme Services, Inc. sales were $7 million annually.

Today Ed is an author, keynote speaker, consultant, coach and mentor to landscape business owners nationwide. He uses his unique "sounding board" approach to act as a silent partner, helping his clients' businesses grow and thrive as a result of his personal mentoring. Ed is a Chartered Certified Landscape Professional (CCLP). He currently sits on the membership committee of the Professional Landcare Network (PLANET), having previously served as an exterior council member.

Ed lives in Wilton, Conn., with his wife and two sons.

FORWARD

America is a place where a person can take their dream and turn it into a highly successful business. I have done it. I began mowing lawns when I was 23 years old and ultimately turned my efforts into a $7 million lawn and landscape business which was later acquired by a national company.

While the ability to realize your dream is real, so are the many challenges and obstacles you will face. Sadly, most start up businesses are destined to fail. Building a lasting and growing business requires drive, determination, guts, persistence, curiosity and some luck. Since no one is born with the total package of business skills and wisdom needed from the start, it is the intent of this book to help equip you with those much needed skills. Every company owner should strive to constantly learn new methods to properly manage people, finances, marketing, regulatory requirements and so much more.

I've written this book for fellow dreamers who are determined to create a successful business. Possessing a dream is the starting point. Your dream might be to start your own company. Or, you might already be in business and desire to take it to a higher level. In the pages of this book, I offer you two valuable benefits:

First, is my experience and perspective as a former business owner who knows firsthand what it takes to build a successful company from scratch, as well as the hurdles that must be overcome as it reaches new stages along the way. The guiding business principles in these pages worked for my company, and can be applied to yours as well. As a consultant I have used them to help other contractors solve problems and achieve their goals. I only wish that I had this book when I started my own company.

Second, this is not a "how to" book with the recipe for success. Owners are unique individuals and so are the companies they build. You cannot build your company by just copying what I did. Instead, in this book I share insights on how successful owners can think and approach problems.

Thinking – the ability to plan and execute the plan – is what separates winners in business from losers. As an owner you're constantly faced with problems and you'll find yourself juggling multiple solutions to each one. While there can be more than one right answer, generally there is only one best approach to take.

This book shares the insight that I gained through my personal experiences, and should enable you to skyrocket your business to growth and profits.

Ed Laflamme

Grass Roots Consulting

INTRODUCTION

Make Money or Get a Job!

Some landscape contractors think they are building a business when the truth is that they are just providing a job for themselves. Put more bluntly, they are selling just enough work needed to earn the wage they are paying themselves and barely breaking even. That's OK if that's their goal, but building a successful business is another matter.

When I started my company, I did not understand business or have a business plan. However, my goal was to create a serious landscape business. Most of the landscape companies I saw didn't do any marketing, they were not good at selling, most had owners who did production work virtually full-time and most didn't even have company uniforms. Company trucks did not even carry the company name on them. Even today, I find companies that have four trucks in all different colors.

What I wanted to build was a successful business that had an identity, that was respected and one in which I wasn't the sole employee. While my vision was not refined, it was dead on for building my business. I knew that I had to hire competent people and delegate to them. I knew I had to learn new things and grow as a businessperson. I accomplished my goal because I saw the vision and was determined to succeed. You can too.

I was asked by a friend of mine to meet with his high school friend because his business was in trouble and he thought I could help. At the meeting I discovered he was at a crossroad in his life – continue with his business or get a job. He told me his revenues were $750,000 in annual sales and he had been in business for 12 years. However, he really wasn't making enough money to justify the hours or the risk. He was working for all general contractors, and every day was a struggle. He had to be low bid in order to get his jobs, and even when the jobs were done it was difficult to get paid.

My advice to him was to change his business model. Some bid work was OK, but not 100 percent. I told him I would be willing to help him, and explained what I thought he needed to do. When I left our meeting I didn't think he had it in him to start over. I found out a few weeks later that he gave up his company and got a job. The sad fact is that his "business" was only worth $70,000 after 12 hard years of work.

Think about that. After 12 years of work – more than 24,000 hours – he had only $70,000 in equity, all from his used equipment. You see he didn't have a vision or a plan. He had always been working for a wage rather than building a business.

Another client is a young guy who had only been in business one year when he hired me. That is unusual, so I asked him why. He told me in our first meeting that he planned to sell his company and retire at 40. I think it's a fantastic plan. He understands that if he builds the company right from the start he will reach his goal. In his third year he is already doing more than $1 million in annual sales and is making a good profit. He is in a good market – balanced between construction and maintenance. He is creating a real business asset in terms of his company and his customer base.

PART 1

Your Business

Chapter	1	The Power of a Plan	19
Chapter	2	The Best Legal Structure	23
Chapter	3	Create a Mastermind Group	25
Chapter	4	The Mower or the Computer	27
Chapter	5	Don't Mess with the IRS	29
Chapter	6	Your Facility	31
Chapter	7	Hire Outside Expertise	35
Chapter	8	Hiring an Accountant	37
Chapter	9	Liability and Insurance	39
Chapter	10	Working with Banks	43

The Power of a Plan

I started mowing grass for money in 1971 and as I mowed I did a lot of thinking. Most commercial mowers then were walk-behinds, so I had plenty of time to think while I walked hour after hour, day after day. My mind would drift at times flooded with so many thoughts. I thanked God to be healthy, free and able to do the type of work I enjoyed. I loved, I mean I really loved working outside in the fresh air, and I loved my new career.

I would think about how great the job would look when it was done and think about how my crew could do the job faster so we could earn more money. I also used to think about how hard it was to get my first group of good customers and keep them happy. I worried about what would happen if I broke my leg or got sick. Would years of hard work go down the drain? The people I had working with me could never run my business. I would lose everything. It was my "aha" moment.

While I mowed, I began to formulate a vision in my mind about how I could avoid potential catastrophe and achieve success. This vision was my first real plan. The only problem was that I didn't write it down. I later learned that a vision not written down is just a dream. When a vision is put in writing only then is it called a plan.

A plan is important because it determines the steps needed to execute your vision. How sad when an owner finally sits down to calculate the company's net worth, only to realize that years of hard work resulted in little to no equity. The balance sheet may show that the only real equity is used vehicles and equipment. That is a sad situation for someone who has worked hard for years, including many 75-hour weeks.

Without a plan, your life is just getting through a series of todays. Success is not just the result of hard work or there would be a lot of rich people. You can't always *work* yourself out of a frustrating situation. You have to *think* your way out. At times you have to be more strategic and less tactical. You need a vision about where you, as a business owner, want to be one day and a detailed supporting plan about how you are going to get there.

The problem with planning is that most owners – including me – have to get to a place where a plan becomes absolutely necessary before we will invest the time and effort needed to write one. Some have to enter encounter problems that only a business plan will help solve before they plan. The power of a written business plan is that it connects all aspects of your business in a logical way that makes it easier to make day-to-day decisions that lead you toward your ultimate goal – a profitable business.

People without formal business training seldom give business planning much thought. I never did. Even those who are educated find it difficult to sit down and map out their future. Most people who start a business do so because they have an idea or see customers with needs they can fill. Some start with a practical working knowledge of the business they go into. Most in the landscape business started mowing lawns while in high school or college as a part-time job or as a way to create a job for themselves. Our business is considered easy-entry. Of course making money in this business, I mean making serious money, is an entirely different matter. For every hundred people who start a landscape business with the best of intentions, only a handful will still be in this line of work 10 years later.

It is incredible to consider the number of people who have either worked for a landscape company while going to school, or who started a landscaping business after school or when they were out of work, only to leave after a short time for some other line of work. Why did they quit? I figure either they didn't like the work or they liked the work, but couldn't make enough money.

I can understand people leaving the business because they don't like the work. It isn't easy, but there is a reason why most landscape contractors love what they do. They love plants, trees, soil and improving God's creation with well-thought out designs. They love improving and maintaining a property beyond even what the owner thought was possible. This gives them a sense of pride and satisfaction. Despite all the business complexities – the weather, the equipment and the people – they persevere.

But it's a shame for anyone who loves this work to have to give it up because they could not make any money. In most cases they didn't make the money they needed simply because they lacked a vision and a plan. Still others love landscaping and stick with it, while barely eking out a living, also because they don't have a plan.

Bruce Crowle, a good friend from Cheshire, Conn., is a living example of the power of a plan. Today, Bruce and his wife Joanne own Atria, one of the premier interior landscape companies in the state. Atria wasn't Crowle's first company. He started a company named Decora in 1974, but without a plan. He was 23 years old, had a degree in biology and loved plants. Within 10 years he decided to sell Decora for various reasons. He then started another company, but this time one thing was different.

"I created a great business plan when I started Atria," Crowle says. "I didn't know much about business, but I went to CompUSA and bought "BizPlan Builder" off the shelf. It was a huge help in getting me started and directing my business thoughts and plans. Amazingly, I went to a local bank and with zero clients and with only my plan in hand, the bank extended us a $25,000 line of credit. The banker said that based on the business plan and our experience in the industry he was confident in lending us the money."

The very act of creating and writing a plan forces you to think. Many do not have a plan because thinking takes time, and they feel it's better to do than to think. Wrong. You need to do both. If you are too busy doing, then you are not thinking. As *E-Myth* author Michael Gerber says in his best seller, entrepreneurs can easily get caught up working in their business rather than on their business. Are you guilty of that? Do you appreciate the difference between the two?

There is a fairly well known saying that goes, "If you fail to plan, plan to fail." So what are you going to do about it? It's never too late to create your business plan. How? Plan to plan. Get your calendar out and set aside one or two days for planning. I strongly suggest engaging the services of a facilitator. Ideally, get someone with green industry experience to help you.

I urge you to develop a written business plan for your company. I did for my company and only wish I had done so years earlier. If you spend some 2,500 hours a year working *in* your company, I am sure you can spare 8 to 16 hours to work *on* your company – to think and plan. My rule of thumb is that you set aside 1 percent of your working time throughout the year to plan for the next 99 percent. Doesn't that make sense?

Review your accomplishments, identify your current situation and present your future vision. Create a SWOT analysis. In other words, analyze your company Strengths, Weaknesses, Opportunities and Threats. Get to know and understand your customers, your competition and your people. Once this is done, create an action plan for the next 12 months and put it in writing. Then, share the plan with your employees to get buy in. Make sure your plan is actionable, visible and your people know what it is. Now execute on it!

There are many "how to" books on writing a business plan, so find one that works for you and use it. You do not need to plan in great detail as some books propose, especially books written for manufacturing companies instead of service businesses. Your plan should cover all the important aspects of your business – goals, budgets, people and marketing – but most importantly your plan needs to be truly useful for you, or you simply won't use it.

One more thing: Refer to your plan at least once a month to make sure you are on course and doing what you decided is necessary to achieve your goals for that year. It's critical to create measurements – benchmarks that determine the success of the plan. For example, did you reach your budget goals for the quarter? Was the percentage of additional sales per month on target? Did you gain the new customer base you expected for the past months according to plan?

Over time, you'll get more comfortable with the process of planning and your plans will evolve, become more detailed and come together more easily. Trust me, business planning is habit forming. A plan gives you direction for the future and many practical insights. So make a commitment to yourself. Get your calendar right now and mark in the dates you will begin to plan.

TAKE ACTION:

- Set aside 1 percent of your working time throughout the year to plan for the next 99 percent.

- Get your calendar out right now and mark down your planning days.

CHAPTER 2

The Best Legal Structure

Putting the right legal business structure in place is a decision that is too important to be left up to a lawyer or CPA. As the owner, you need to know your options and make a smart decision about which one is best for you. All have some trade-offs. The question is which one is best?

For example, let's say you want to sell your business and retire in five years. If you were established as a C-Corporation you are facing double taxation. When you take a check from the buyer (new owner) your corporation will be taxed and then when you take your money out of the corporation you will be taxed. Altogether you and your company will pay a combined tax of more than 50 percent!

During a conversation with a client I learned that his CPA set him up as a C-Corporation. I contacted the accountant and asked him why he chose this structure. There was silence on the other end of the phone. In order to avoid double taxation and create greater equity for my client we changed the company's corporate structure.

Let's take the mystery out of this right now. In the United States the five basic options are: Sole Proprietorship, LLC, S-Corp or C-Corp and General Partnerships. There are also some specialized types of partnerships, but most small business use one of these five structures. In order to create the largest equity (cash value) in your company you need the right entity. So how do you know which one to choose?

Many are turning to the Internet using online services to select and start a corporation. It's fast and cheap. Others go to an accountant or lawyer and take whatever advice they are given without understanding the ramifications. I agree with the Professional Landcare Network's (PLANET) attorney, Chip Watkins of Chamberlain, Webster & Bean in Washington, DC. Watkins told me, "Internet sites offer a cookie-cutter approach and don't take into consideration the circumstances of each individual. It would be better to deal with a local attorney that would walk you carefully through all of your options. But caution should be used in selecting the professionals one uses for their business."

In selecting one of the five entities, it's key to know the four areas of concern: protection of assets, flexibility with regard to owners' perks, tax advantages and equity creation. A fifth consideration is your basic motive for starting a company – is it to build and sell after a period of time, or are you building a company to pass on to future generations?

Even if you have been in business for a time you may want to change the structure to gain important advantages. Don't be left wondering if your structure is the right one. Get answers to your questions from a good attorney and/or CPA. Arrange to meet with them and review your circumstances. Cover the options listed above until you come to consensus on how to move forward. Once you take the mystery out of this you can move forward with confidence knowing that your structure supports your vision.

TAKE ACTION:

- If you are not positive you currently have the correct business structure, have professionals review it to be sure.

CHAPTER 3

Create A Mastermind Group

Early in my business career a business executive gave me a copy of *Think & Grow Rich* by Napoleon Hill. The book is a must-read for every businessperson. The story behind this book is about how people become rich. Andrew Carnegie, who had become the richest man in the world, became interested in better understanding how the rich got there. Carnegie engaged the services of Napoleon Hill to research dozens of his wealthy friends to see what the super rich had in common. It took Hill 20 years to complete the book. The young Hill, having met this elite group and following the principles they shared, himself eventually became part of this wealth group.

I bring this book up because one of the chapters is titled, "The Mastermind Group." In this chapter Hill describes how all of the super wealthy had a "mastermind group" – people carefully selected by a future "Mr. Big Bucks" for their diverse talents and expertise. The rich made it a practice to meet with their mastermind groups on a regular basis to discuss a variety of subjects. Call it an "advisory board," "dream team" or "brain trust" if you like, but these people provided balance and sage advice.

Why not consider such a group for yourself or your company? Please don't confuse a mastermind group with a board of directors. A board of directors offers advice, yes, but they have certain liabilities, are generally compensated for their services and usually focus their attention directly on the business. With a mastermind group we are talking about people who offer advice that is more centered on helping the person i.e., their career development as well as their business and investments. Usually the people in such a group have "made it" and offer advice in how to "make it" as well.

If the super rich and super successful rely on such a group, wouldn't it be a good idea to imitate them? Many successful people recognize that they can't achieve everything they want entirely by themselves. They – and we – need a resource, a forum to gain perspective, a place to seek advice from the wise, a safe place to reveal our dreams, our problems, our motives and our ambitions. And, aside from this sage advice, these people can help open business doors. How valuable is that?

Most independent business owners are free spirits and not always as open-minded as they should be. The entrepreneurial spirit is an awesome quality but let's face reality, you don't know what you don't know. The person on the ground that never climbed the mountain cannot have the same perspective as the person who has already climbed to the top. Before you begin your ascent or climb without a clear plan, wouldn't it be beneficial to have people around you who have already been there?

No matter what your area of expertise and talents in a specific business area, it is nearly impossible to have the breadth and depth of expertise in every business area. To run a landscape business you have to know something about banking, accounting, finance, law, human resources, horticulture, computing, mechanics, purchasing, human relations and on and on. Determine your area of expertise and turn to experts to fill in the gaps.

If you don't have a mastermind group I urge you to consider creating one. This group can help you avoid the pitfalls and problems that are common to new owners and move your company along faster than you ever could have imagined. You can't be successful by yourself so why not assemble your own mastermind group to help you achieve success?

TAKE ACTION:

- Consider assembling a mastermind group to help guide you and your business.

CHAPTER 4

The Mower or the Computer?

Without question, landscape contractors try to purchase the best equipment they can afford for their crews. Quality tools and equipment enable crews to be more efficient. The same is true for office equipment. However, in my experience, I find that business owners tend to go cheap when buying office equipment. They feel it's more important to invest in a new mower than a new computer. So, in many cases, computer hardware and software is outdated and unsupported and office staff just has to deal with it, creating handicaps rather than enabling office efficiency.

Since computers are not my field, I decided I'd better get some help. I consulted a computer expert. Her answer to my opening question on purchasing hardware and software was, "When purchasing software there are two costs: the license fee and support and maintenance. These costs are based on your annual agreement. For obvious reasons, all software running on the computers in your organization should have a valid license." If the reasons are not obvious to you, here's the deal: Without proper licens-es you can't get upgrades and support if you have problems with the software. And of course, it's illegal.

She continues, "When deciding on software maintenance agreements, you should ensure that appropriate version upgrades, security patches and support are included. Also, before the purchase has been made is the best time to think about and create an implementation plan."

What great advice. Two of my clients not aware of this criteria, failed to "think out and plan" their software purchase. The result is an implementation lasting more than two years, going on three with a cost of four times the original software price. So, the moral of the story, is know what you're getting into before the purchase.

With regard to the best method of implementation she told me, "Is there a staff member well-versed in the software who can easily implement it within your company? If not, you may be wise to get assistance from the supplier. Generally, financial accounting systems and customer relationship management software tend to require implementation expertise.

Your supplier can either provide this directly or refer you to someone in your local area."

I asked how companies should evaluate their computer needs, especially as they grow. She said, "Computer hardware and software support should also be evaluated based upon your business requirements. If your company is larger, your computer needs will grow over time. Your office staff should be able to leverage the full functionality of the software you have implemented, while ensuring a positive end-user experience. Support and training go hand-in-hand and can be provided by either the software supplier or a computer consultant." More great advice, so don't hesitate to contact a computer expert to help you evaluate your needs and offer guidance.

Her final words of advice to business owners is, "as your business requirements grow, evolve and change so too will your office hardware and software requirements. Be true to the value proposition you are gaining from each purchase and ensure it is in line with your overall objectives.

Value proposition? What she is saying is be sure that you are fully using both your software and hardware so your investment in these tools pays off and is fully accomplishing the results you intended.

TAKE ACTION:

- Don't skimp on good quality office equipment.

- Stay up-to-date with the latest computers and software and be sure they are supported by the company you purchased them from.

CHAPTER 5

Don't Mess with the IRS!

You know the old adage that you can't avoid death and taxes. This is true but the smart landscape contractor pays only the taxes he absolutely must. When you first begin your business paying taxes is not on your mind. Rather, your only thought is making a profit. But once your business grows and makes money, paying taxes can become a real problem, a "high class" problem as one friend of mine used to say, especially if you have not done any tax planning.

Believe it or not paying taxes is the right thing and the smart thing to do. During the 30 years I was in business there were many owners who avoided paying taxes by accepting as much cash "off the books" from customers as they could. There are many problems with that practice. First of all it's illegal. Secondly, it is not as profitable as it might first appear considering most customers want a discount if they are paying with cash. Third and most important, owners who don't record all their income on their books can't show the level of profit *and sales* needed to get banks to extend credit to help them grow. And when it comes time to sell the business, the buyer and the bank will only consider the numbers "on the books," not what you say the company really did.

One example I would like to share with you was a landscape company owner who asked me to help him sell his company. Average sales for his last three years were $1.5 million dollars. After reviewing his books and talking to him he revealed he was taking cash from customers of more than $200,000 per year. I asked him what he was doing with the cash. He explained he was using most of it for overtime and bonuses for his people. He said he had started this practice years ago and it had grown until it was a real "monkey on his back."

What a liability he had created for himself. Income tax evasion, liability with the state, federal, tax and unemployment departments. Yikes. Facing possible jail time if discovered, he was scared and wanted to get out. Many owners take *some* cash, but $200,000 a year? He was in a pickle. How does he explain this to a potential buyer – would you want this liability if you bought his business?

Most of the owners who "take

cash" don't put the money into a Swiss bank account. Most use it to purchase boats, cars and other toys or they use this money to pay their people bonuses or pay for the overtime worked, as described above. They are not building equity in their companies because they take most all the profit out and spend it. As a result, a number of these owners are still working in the field with their crews because they simply can't afford not to be. It's not a good position to be in after working hard in your business for 10, 20 or more years.

If you are going to play the "game of landscaping" at the "pro" level, then play to win and accept the fact that you will be paying taxes. I certainly am not advocating you pay "Uncle Sam" a dollar more than is required. That's why good tax planning is so very important.

As part of the planning process, keep good business records and have a good bookkeeping system. My advice is to get help on this and on your tax planning from the professional team you have assembled. If you are an LLC or a Sub S corporation, use the tax advantages that these corporate structures allow to the fullest.

TAKE ACTION:

- Pay the taxes for which you are legally obligated so you can sleep at night.

- Tax evasion is illegal, tax avoidance is not, work with professionals to avoid paying unnecessary taxes.

CHAPTER 6

Your Facility

Most landscape business owners began by working out of their home or apartment. I started this way until my father-in-law's one-bay garage was exploding with my equipment. From there I purchased a three-car garage on an empty lot in a scary part of the city. At the time I didn't care where it was, I was just happy to have the additional room (and my father-in-law was happy to reclaim his garage). Like a chef needs a kitchen and a surgeon needs his operating room, your landscape business needs a home. Without a good home it is difficult to build a solid business that will one day hold value.

Where should you buy or lease your home? It all depends on where your customers are, where your employees live and how much property costs in your area. I believe the most important factor is to locate your facility in a place most convenient to your employees. If you purchase a place where your customers are it may feed your ego but will your employees be able to get there? Locating in an area closer to your employees may mean some "windshield time" in traveling to serve customers, but chalk that up to the price of doing business. I know some very successful companies, with double-digit net profits, that travel up to one hour each morning to reach their customer base. Give considerable thought to where your new "home" will be. Home base will have a major bearing on the success of your business going forward.

There are three important questions to consider before buying or leasing a property:

1. Will the land serve the company for the long-term?
2. Will the property grow in value and be saleable in the future?
3. Will the overhead be too much to make sense?

Let's take a look at each of these questions. To start be sure to purchase a piece of property that will accommodate your short- and long-term needs. I have more than one client looking for property because their current property is not conducive to growth. Property has a way of shrinking as you grow so you may consider purchasing more now even if it's a bit of a stretch. If you are leasing and not buying, find out the potential of leasing more space as you grow before the lease is signed.

If you are going to buy, be sure the property value will grow over time. Although the property will serve the needs of the business it is still an investment and you want to eventually make a return on the investment. Before committing, carefully research the neighborhood. If it's going downhill you could be in trouble in the future. Professionals in real estate can help you make this determination. Your local bankers can offer advice as well. Ask them if they would be willing to finance you if you purchased property in the neighborhood you are considering. And a few hours invested in speaking to your potential new neighbors wouldn't hurt either.

It is important to select the right property if you plan to sell your business or have your children take it over. Be sure it will be in the type of neighborhood that is safe and will work in the future.

Lastly, be sure the deal makes sense. More than one of my friends has leased a property because they felt it was in a great location but it ended up increasing their overhead so much it that it prevented the business from really making a strong profit. Another contractor I know overbuilt on a large piece of property he had purchased. He visited contractors all over the country so he could design the best facility possible. He built a fantastic place but there was downturn in the economy the following year. He didn't make his projected sales and his company went into a tailspin. This expensive facility ultimately forced him into bankruptcy.

Let's learn from this lesson. Ideally you want to buy property to build equity. If you must lease understand that you are not creating equity. Set a goal to purchase property as soon as it is possible. The real estate that becomes the home for your business can generate substantial future profits. If you decide to sell your business in the future you can either sell or lease back the property to the potential buyer. Either way you win.

TAKE ACTION:

- As soon as you can afford it purchase property to serve as a "home" for your business.

- Be sure the location of the business property works for your employees and customers.

- Purchase property in an area where there will be future appreciation.

- Your new purchase may be a stretch, but don't let it bury you if your sales turn down.

CHAPTER 7

Hire Outside Expertise

Attorneys, accountants, consultants and other professional advisers cost money, but they can be a wise investment. My experience has shown it's more expensive over time not seeking professional help when you need it than saving a few dollars in the near term. A word of caution, be sure you have the right pros on your team. Let me share one of my experiences.

Once an age discrimination lawsuit was brought against my company. During the winter we lost three good-sized jobs, so that spring we did not rehire the people we used for those jobs. During the new season we worked hard to replace the lost jobs and by mid-summer we had replaced them all. One of the men we didn't rehire went to the Equal Employment Opportunities Council (EEOC) and filed suit against us. He was over 40 years old. He claimed he was discriminated against because of his age. Truthfully, we hired the best people we could for the new contract work. We thought it best to let him collect unemployment and find another job.

I spoke to my corporate attorney, whom I had on retainer, about the case. He said not to worry. The EEOC summoned us to what they called an "informal hearing." If you ever find yourself in this situation know that there is no such thing as an "informal" hearing because everything said becomes a matter of formal record and can and most likely will be used against you later. Anyway, I went to the hearing with my corporate attorney. The former employee wanted an undetermined amount of money to settle. Actually he was waiting for me to make a settlement offer. Not feeling I was in the wrong, and not knowing I was in violation of the law, I stuck to my guns and chose to go to the next step, a formal hearing.

Again, my attorney said not to worry. Looking back, that's when I really should have started worrying. On the day of the hearing, I was called as a witness and when questioned as to why we did not rehire this man I responded that we did not feel his work was up to par and chose to hire another person. The attorney I had retained was not a "labor specialist" and he didn't know that in this situation I was required by law to rehire the man. I was totally unaware that I had to rehire those I had laid off before hiring new people. I was looking at losing the case and possibly owing $250,000 in damages.

I immediately contacted a labor attorney, explained my situation and asked for his help. He took over the case and I asked my corporate attorney to step aside. The result: the labor attorney got me out of the mess and we settled for a few thousand dollars, but not after spending close to $50,000 in legal fees with the new attorney.

The moral of the story is to hire the best employees and professionals to begin with. They will serve as a better investment in the long run. Also, if a person is fired because of poor performance or other reasons don't, lay them off. Fire them for cause.

When assembling your professional team determine their value. Don't get hung up on hourly rates, value and impact you will get from their experience and knowledge. I have found that the professionals who charge the most have the greatest knowledge and get the job done faster, better and cheaper.

Include business consultants as part of your pro team. I used the best in the industry when I was in business and most gave me insight that I was unable to glean any other way.

When I was in business for just a few years I took a course on basic horticulture. I was so impressed with the teacher's knowledge that I hired him as a consultant for the company. This relationship lasted 25 years. I also used financial, strategic, and operational specialists. I always felt that the money I spent on these experts was a wise investment.

Consulting experts include your CPA, attorney, business consultant and successful business friends. They will help you avoid the roadblocks and pitfalls in business and move you down the road to achieving your vision.

TAKE ACTION:

- Assemble the best group of professionals you can possibly afford; they will be less expensive in the long run and serve you better.

- Do whatever you can to avoid litigation; it is distracting to your business, your personal life and usually - only the attorneys win.

CHAPTER 8

Hiring an Accountant

Right from the beginning of your business I recommend finding and working with an accountant, preferably a CPA (Certified Public Accountant). Talk to more than one before you make a hiring decision. Once you interview several you will find out that accounting jargon is about all they share in common – terms like "balance sheet, cash flow, overhead" and the like. What is surprising is that beyond these basic terms accountants may differ sharply on what they can do for you and how they will do it. A good accountant can help you get your business off to a solid start. It's smart to hire one right from the start, even though you may not think you can afford to.

When it comes to hiring an accountant, or even doing your own books, it is critical that your bookkeeping system be one that you fully understand and that meets your needs. If you don't like a system you won't fully adopt it. You should determine if you are getting the numbers you are expecting to see out of your system. When you hire an accountant, tell him or her which reports are important to you and in what format they should be. You should also know how often you want to run your reports in order to get meaningful and useful information. Since you are paying for your financial statements you should clearly describe what information you want and what data you need in order to make the right financial decisions for your company. Have the accountant explain your options. Then agree upon what your requirements are.

If you are already working with an accountant and the reports they are producing aren't clear and useable, talk to them about changing the reports in order to produce the information you need. If, after a frank discussion they don't want to change, you may consider hiring someone else who will work for you and do the job to meet your needs. I can't overemphasize this point. You are the client. You make financial decisions based on the information and data you are receiving from your accountant. Never delegate the entire responsibility or oversight of your business finances to any other person. If you give up control of your financial reports, you can lose control of your entire business.

What should you look for in an accountant? A person or company that can help you grow your company by saving you money and that understands business and not just how to do tax returns. Accounting should not be just an added cost of doing business. It should help build your profits by enabling you to cut expenses, reduce taxes, price your work correctly and make smarter business decisions.

Do you need to hire a certified public accountant (CPA)? Not necessarily but at least their equivalent. I have found that an experienced Certified Management Accountant (CMA) can be as good as or even better than a CPA because they specialize in company systems and processes. The CPA usually specializes in taxes.

What's most important is that the person you work with understands your service business, offers you options and advice and works in your company's best interests.

TAKE ACTION:

- As soon as possible hire an accountant to organize your books.

- A CPA or their equivalent is important, but equally important is their understanding of business.

- Get involved with your accountant and learn how to read P & L's, balance sheets and reports that help you run your business profitably.

CHAPTER 9

Liability and Insurance

W hat do you mean I'm not covered? I thought I had a comprehensive policy?"

"Yes, but your policy does not cover an employee who drives his car onto one of your customer's properties and causes damage. That coverage should come from your employee's car insurance. If he was driving your vehicle and not his own you would have been covered."

Most insurance policies are broad enough to cover most situations, but no policy eliminates all liability. In the case described above I learned too late that my employee had no insurance on his car and I was stuck with the $7,500 bill for the brand new light pole he knocked over on a construction job. The ironic part of this story is the added coverage didn't cost anything; it was added at no additional premium cost.

After some research I discovered that there is a niche of professionals who have started independent companies that will review your policies for a fee. Recently one of my clients brought in one of these companies. Wow, were they shocked. These consultants not only saved them three

times their fee, but found a huge hole in their coverage. They even negotiated the premium the insurance company was going to charge for the next year. Negotiate the premium, really? Yes. And another thing, ask your agent to separate the agency fee from the insurance company's premium and they can be both negotiable.

If you can't afford or you are not large enough to hire one of these consultants you can certainly have competitive agents and companies review your existing policies for their input. It's amazing how many problems another agent can find and take care of when they want your business.

There are two types of liabilities, those you can avoid and those you can't. The most costly claims are the avoidable but for which you have no insurance coverage. Many incidents fall into this category, but the big three are environmental, safety and personnel claims. There are comprehensive laws on the books that cover your responsibilities as an employer for environmental, safety and personnel claims. Become familiar with them. As any judge will tell you, ignorance is no excuse.

When considering the area of environmental liability you should know how you and your people handle chemicals. Do the employees using chemicals have the proper licensing or certification and documented training? If they injure themselves or others you may be personally liable. Do you know what your applicators are doing with leftover chemicals? Are your chemicals stored legally? Where does your used oil go from small equipment and trucks? Whether you have a company pick up your used oil or you bring it to a recycling center get a receipt and keep it on file to prove the oil was disposed of properly.

Be proactive and tell your local fire department or the fire marshal where and what chemicals are stored on your premises. Some communities have laws requiring such notification. In the case of a fire you could be held liable if a fireman was injured from fumes or explosions and you were not in compliance with these regulations. Many of the companies I visit for the first time are in obvious violation of local, state or federal laws.

Regarding safety liabilities, ask yourself how safety conscious is your company? If a person were seriously injured on the job, how would help be called? Do you hold regular safety meetings and have appointed a safety director? One solution some companies use is to hold weekly 10-minute tailgate training meetings.

How would your company do in an OHSA inspection? In many locations there are public agencies that will inspect your operation at no charge and give you a comprehensive report regarding compliance action needed. The only obligation you have is to get in full compliance after the inspection. This can be very important, as I learned in my business.

One day an accident occurred that I hope none of you ever have to face. While delivering flowers to a parking garage one of my employees was killed. The truck he was riding in had a space between the cab and racks. For no apparent reason he jumped up onto this platform without the driver knowing it. While standing on the platform he was caught between the steel girder on the garage roof and the racks of the truck as it moved forward, only at some five miles per hour. People watching screamed for him to get down but it was too late and it was over in seconds. His head was caught between the steel ceiling beam and the truck racks. He fell off the truck, lifeless. We were all devastated.

You can imagine what happened as a result of this accident. OSHA was there immediately to investigate. If I had not been proactive in seeking full compliance prior to the accident the OSHA fines could have put us out of business. You see, they not only investigated the accident but also checked all of my 50 some trucks, my offices and two shops. The result of their investigation showed absolutely no fault on our part yet they still managed to fine me $5,000 for miscellaneous violations.

Personnel liability is another area you should fully understand along with the laws to be sure you are in compliance. There are laws regarding, hiring, firing, sexual harassment, age and other types of discrimination and, of course, federal and state wage and hour laws. Get familiar with the requirements and get professional help if you need it. Insurance is a necessary evil, be sure you have proper coverages and are paying the lowest price for it.

TAKE ACTION:

• Consider hiring an independent insurance consultant to review your policies or at least prior to the end of your policy year have other agents or companies review them not only for pricing but also for proper coverage.

• Be proactive and have your property inspected to be sure you are in OSHA compliance.

• Be sure your agent puts your policy out to bid with other insurance companies every renewal period.

CHAPTER 10

Working with Banks

It didn't take me long to appreciate the fact that banks like to loan money to people and companies that don't actually need it, but not to those who do need it. At least that is how I felt when they turned me down for loans in my early years. This is especially painful when your company is growing and needs cash. The key is to establish bank relationships when you don't need them. I also recommend that you have a relationship with more than one bank.

I think it's good to work with a big bank and a small local community bank. Borrow from both. Let each know that you have a relationship with other banks and not just them. Their rates will be better and so will their service.

In the 30 years I was in business, a number of banks I worked with were sold, merged or went out of business because of bad loans. Having a second bank prevented these transitions from putting a severe strain on my company. One close friend of mine had a single bank relationship and was almost put out of business because the bank called in his cash line because of a merger.

Banks are businesses made up of people, so invite your bankers to lunch. Visit them. Keep them in the loop about what is happening with your company. They don't like surprises, so if you have a problem, tell them. Then show them your written business plans and make them feel warm and fuzzy.

In the stock market crash October of 1987, my bank was in trouble because of bad real estate loans. They needed cash and needed it fast because the FDIC was breathing down their back. As a result they contacted me and other company owners to call in our cash lines. It was in the middle of my season and I didn't have the money to pay them. I didn't have a strong relationship with another bank at the time, so I called my CPA for help. I met with a banker he recommended.

We immediately provided her with everything they wanted, from P&L statements, budgets and cash flow projections. The paperwork was a foot high. After a few meetings, she agreed to take over the cash line from my bank. I will never will forget the day of the closing. I was not in default with the other bank but it was getting close. The banker and I were in the waiting room of the bank's attorneys. I learned that day why they called it a waiting room. We waited and I sweated. We waited and I sweated some more.

I could tell the banker was losing patience with her attorney. She said maybe we should reschedule for another day. I tried to make small talk. Finally the moment of truth came. She was beginning to have second thoughts. If she backed out at this point I would be in a mess. She was sitting at a right angle to me, and I will never forget how she quietly yet firmly leaned over and moved into my personal space. At about 12 inches from my face she said, "Ed, are you going to be able to repay this loan?" My mouth went dry. I locked eyes with her and with as much confidence as I could muster replied, "Absolutely, I have never in 17 years defaulted or

even been late on a loan payment." She continued to look me right in the eye, leaned back and straightened up and said, "Let me see what is taking that attorney so long." When she stood up the attorney walked in the room. That was a moment of truth for me, and what a lesson I learned.

Bankers try to negotiate the highest interest rates they can get. If they know you and become your friend, they are likely to be reasonable and get you a loan at competitive rates. It's up to you to get your best deal. Don't feel that you are at their mercy. Banks can be fickle. Sometimes they want your business, other times their people and policies change and then they don't. Shop around. Establish lines of credit when you don't need them. If you think you might need a line of credit for $100,000 work to get $150,000. Money is like oxygen. When you don't have quite enough, your business dies.

TAKE ACTION:

- Form relationships with more than one bank and borrow from both.

- Borrow and establish lines of credit with banks when you don't need the money.

- Don't fall in love with one bank, shop for the best terms and interest rate.

PART 2

Your Money

Chapter	1	Profit is Not a Dirty Word	47
Chapter	2	The Boss is Getting Rich	49
Chapter	3	Keeping Score	51
Chapter	4	Your P&L Gives You the Score	53
Chapter	5	The Rule of 10	57
Chapter	6	The Chart of Accounts - Backbone of Your P&L	59
Chapter	7	Pricing – Critical to Your Success	63
Chapter	8	Pricing – Be Accurate & Consistent	65
Chapter	9	Pricing – Your Markup Options	67
Chapter	10	Estimating 101	69
Chapter	11	Job Costing is Not an Option!	71
Chapter	12	What – No Budget?	75
Chapter	13	Invoice 'Em Early	77
Chapter	14	Train Them to Pay – On Time!	79
Chapter	15	Better Have Good Contracts	81
Chapter	16	Money – Checks & Controls	85

CHAPTER 1

Profit is Not a Dirty Word

Cash flow is the lifeblood of a company, but if you are not making a profit your business will not survive. Because of this fact, profit must never be a negative word for you or your employees. Profit is not a dirty word. Many employees think the owner gouges the poor customer and takes home 50 cents out of every dollar they charge. Someone riding a mower knows how much they are being paid per hour, how much gas costs and probably how much the customer is paying. Add this up and it can look like a lot of money is being made by somebody – you. What the mower operator does not know is the cost of sales and marketing, callbacks, insurance, rent, bank payments, taxes and all the other overhead items involved in running a business.

What owners often fail to realize is that on top of all the costs, including their own compensation, the business is also entitled to a profit – that's why the business exists.

Here's another way of looking at the subject. As the owner, you should not consider yourself *the* business. You are a working contributor to the business and entitled to your fair pay and benefits. Above and beyond this, the business is also entitled to a profit. Profit is necessary to pay unexpected bills and to invest in future growth. Consider this, if you decided tomorrow to sell all of the assets of your company and then take that money and invest it in stocks or cash deposits (CDs), the invested money would earn you a return on your money. Now, if you decide to stay in business, those same assets should be earning you a return far greater than you would get from stocks or interest-bearing CDs. Why? The risk. It's your neck that's on the line with the banks, vendors and dealers. So the company needs to earn a profit after your salary and all overhead.

Some reading this might think that the above advice is great for someone else, but they are barely paying the bills as is. If this is the case, figure out what the problem is. Not enough sales, too much overhead, under pricing, inaccurate estimating, whatever. My suggestion is to get help. Create a profit plan. Start working on your business so you can make a healthy profit, or you may want to consider moving on.

TAKE ACTION:

- Profit is not a dirty word. Explain to all of your people how much it costs to operate the company and that profit is needed for its ongoing growth.

- The company should be making a profit after you – the owner – takes a fair salary.

- Create a "profit plan" for your company.

- If you're stuck, get outside help.

CHAPTER 2

The Boss is Getting Rich

As the owner it's your right to keep your books confidential if you wish. But it is important to educate your people about the cost of doing business. I have always practiced this philosophy on a need-to-know basis. Some need to know others don't. Some companies operate with an "open book" management approach – they share income, costs and profit information with employees. The first time I heard about this was at a Professional Landcare Network (PLANET) event. Robert Stack, author of *The Great Game of Business*, explained how powerful open book management had been in his company. A few years later John Case, a writer I know from Inc. Magazine, became interested in the subject and subsequently wrote a book called, *Open Book Management*. John's book is excellent if you want to learn more about how this philosophy can be used in your company.

What do your people need to understand about profit? First, their jobs depend on it. Second, profit fuels debt reduction, investment and future growth. Third, profit margins are never as big as people think.

Fourth, employees' actions every day on the job have a huge impact on the bottom line. Every dollar saved on the job is a dollar that should drop right to the bottom line.

Your employees need to understand the basic facts of business life. They may think that the boss is getting rich because all they see is the direct cost of running a job. They need to understand that in our industry direct job costs eat up about half of every sales dollar. Then they need to learn how almost all of the balance is used up to cover company overhead and that less than they think goes to the owner – especially when owners risk, investment and time is taken into consideration. One owner I know in a company wide meeting used a powerful illustration to demonstrate the expenses in his business. He had 100 pennies and gave them all to one of his Hispanic workers. He then went through ever single line item of his P&L. Of course, the last item was profit. The laborer had 3 cents left! They were all blown away. This little exercise changed the attitude of everyone. Subsequently they all worked much harder for the company. Would this type of exercise help illustrate the point in your company?

To finish up on this subject, no you don't have to tell your people how much you pay yourself or what other bonuses you take out. They don't need to know that. But, teach your people that productivity and cost control have a huge impact on profit. And, that profit is absolutely necessary.

TAKE ACTION:

- Educate your people about the huge costs of operating a company.

- Consider the "100 penny" illustration to demonstrate where all the money goes.

CHAPTER 3

Keeping Score!

People in America are taught that it's not polite to talk about money, but money is one of business' key indicators. It's the way you keep score, and in that respect it's a measure of success.

One person might start a company with the goal of becoming independently wealthy in 10 years, while another just wants to earn enough money to be able to work four days a week and fish or golf the other three days. Regardless of your reason for starting a business, if your company is not profitable, you will soon be out of business. It's just that simple.

Books addressing all aspects of money in business are available. From budgeting to tracking cash flow and profit, these books cover business subjects in-depth, I suggest you find, buy and read several. But right now let me help you get grounded on some key principles.

In order to have success in your business, it's necessary to have a good "handle" on the flow of money in and out of your company. You need to know what happened in the past and be able to predict with some certainty what's coming next week, next month and next year. True, this is a simple concept, but few business owners actually track money properly until it becomes a survival issue. What I mean by "track money" is to simply pay attention to the basics. Ask yourself at the end of each month, do you know what your sales were, how much money you now owe, if you're making money on your jobs, what your labor cost is as a percentage of sales, etc.?

As an owner you can manage business finances with a pencil, a bookkeeping ledger and two shoe boxes – one for income and one for payments. Many huge companies started out exactly this way. And, if your company is a start-up, you don't necessarily need an expensive computer and complicated software to track your finances. In fact, the cost to buy a computer and the time needed to learn how to use the software could be a barrier against actually taking the time to track your finances. You probably enjoy creating landscapes, cutting grass and keeping turf in top condition more than trying to learn to use new financial software. But whether you use paper and a pencil or a computer, the important point is that you must keep score.

Know where your business finances are today, tomorrow and always.

TAKE ACTION:

- You don't need an expensive computer or financial system, but you do need to keep score of your income and expenses on a monthly basis.

CHAPTER 4

Your P&L Gives You The Score

Do you know if you are making money in your business? Do you know what your break-even is? Do you know what your overhead is each day? To operate a profitable and successful business you need to know all of this. Your income statement, also known as the profit and loss (P&L) statement is one good way to "keep score" in your business.

Many business owners do not know the answers to the above questions. Think about it, can you imagine a pro football or baseball team not keeping score as they play the game? Pro teams are obsessed with scores and statistics.

I am amazed at how many companies "play the game of business" without keeping score. Some get their "score" four to five months after the game has ended because they need the "numbers" at tax time. Others impatiently wait for their accountant to tell them at the end of their calendar year if they "won or lost." No one in sports would play a game like that, and no one should run a business like that either.

I believe many business owners don't get a monthly P&L statement because they don't see the value in it. They wrongly believe the effort and cost to create a P&L will not impact the final outcome at the end of the year. Others simply don't know how to do it, so they just keep playing the game fast and furious, believing it doesn't matter. If you are either one of these owners, I can only urge you to reconsider. I guess if you work by yourself, or have one or two employees, and never hope to build equity in your business, grow it or sell it, then there might not be much point to a P&L statement. But, if you have other aspirations, then it's time to put the systems in place so you know where your company is headed at all times.

If you want to grow, if you want to be profitable, if you want to build equity in your company, then you need accurate and timely (monthly) P&L statements. When I say timely, I mean it's important to get your P&L as soon as possible once your month is closed. With this information on hand you can react to any problem or negative trend that might be developing. If you have an outside accounting firm generate your P&L, give them a reasonable schedule, mutually agreed upon, and hold them to it. Take no excuses, period. I suggest having your P&L complete by the 15th of the month for the past month, so you should know exactly how you did in April by May 15th.

Whether you call them income statements, profit and loss statements or P&Ls, this report keeps score. It identifies if you are winning or losing in business. It shows what your revenue is by profit center, what your costs are, how much overhead your company has and how much profit or loss has been made. Income statements have a 12-month cycle, called the company's fiscal year that can begin when ever you want. In my consulting practice I have seen statements begin on months other than January. Regardless of the date it should make sense to you as it pertains to the operation of your business, and not for the convenience of your accountant.

Another thing I notice when looking at P&L statements for a new client is that many times they don't print the percentages next to the numbers. Be sure that all of your statements always include percentages. Raw numbers don't mean anything unless you know what the relative relationships are. To make the point: a $100,000 net profit might seem good if you are a $1 million company (that represents a 10 percent net profit). But if you are running a $10 million company, that same $100,000 means you are earning only a 1 percent net profit!

Lastly, if you have created a chart of accounts then you can also purchase from PLANET a publication entitled, *Operating Cost Study*. The information in this report is extremely valuable so you can compare your company with others of similar size, business type and geographic location. When I first purchased this cost study years ago, it alerted me that my insurance costs seemed high. This led me to get pricing from another agent. The result was a savings of $22,000 that first year – a good return on investment for a book that cost less than $50.

If you don't receive a monthly P&L, it's time to begin. If you are receiving one, be sure to take the time to analyze the results so you know if you are winning or losing.

TAKE ACTION:

- If you are going to play the game of business keep score monthly with your P & L so you know how you're doing.

- Insist that the P & L's are complete by the 15th of the following month for the past month. Carefully review them so you know the direction of the company.

- Write percentages beside all totals on the P&L, these will become key indicators as to the health of the company.

CHAPTER 5

The Rule of 10

The Rule of 10 is a simple but powerful concept. If any department of your company equals 10 percent or more of your annual sales, then that department should have its own mini financial statement. What I mean is the sales and expenses for these departments should be tracked separately so you know what the gross profit or gross margin is.

For those of you reading this without much knowledge of financial terms I strongly suggest you purchase the book, *Pricing for the Green Industry* by Frank Ross. This publication can be obtained from PLAN-ET. Many consider this "the bible" for landscapers in the business. This publication describes what comprises "direct costs", how to arrive at the gross margin and how your chart of accounts needs to be structured to arrive at these numbers.

The main point behind this rule is that every revenue-generating department will have a different gross margin and that if the department is a significant part of the total sales of the company it is important to know if the department is achieving their gross margin.

If you do not track each business department separately then your profitable departments may be carrying your less profitable or even money-losing departments. For example, I started my business doing landscape maintenance work. Later I added construction and then snow plowing. As I added these services, on I lumped them together under sales.

I brought in a consultant, and the first two things he looked at were my pricing and my profit and loss statements. Since both my construction and snow departments had revenue above 10 percent of my total, he suggested a separate budget and P&L for all three departments – maintenance, construction and snow. I took his advice and quickly learned that my construction profits were far lower than what I had believed. That meant maintenance and snow work were subsidizing my construction department. This discovery enabled me to take action and adjust my pricing structure.

If a department in your company produces less than 10 percent of your revenue then it is probably not necessary to track it separately. If a department is less than 10 percent then most likely that departments overall impact is probably not that great. As an example, if your annual revenue is $500,000 and you did tree work totally $25,000.00 it doesn't warrant the extra paperwork to track that separately.

TAKE ACTION:

- Once a department reaches 10 percent of the gross sales of the company it should be tracked separately.

- Purchase *Pricing for the Green Industry* by Frank Ross.

CHAPTER 6

The Chart of Accounts – Backbone of Your P&L

I was in business for eight years before I even heard the term chart of accounts. Lacking a formal business or accounting education, my first attempt at learning about the numbers aspect of business was at a Ross Payne Associates seminar in Chicago in 1980. It was a two-day seminar packed with information on profit and loss statements, budgets and wealth-building ideas for small business owners.

My head ached at the end of the first day but I began to understand the value of "keeping score" with P&Ls and how to do it. The purpose of this chapter is not to offer an accounting course, but rather to raise your awareness of the need for the right chart of accounts and why it's so important.

A chart of accounts is really nothing more than a listing of the categories of accounts in your accounting system. It tracks by category your income and expense so you know where your money came from (sales) and where it went (expenses). If you operate your business without really knowing where your money goes, it's time for change. Creating a solid chart of accounts is a big step in getting your financial house in order.

There are two main categories in a chart of accounts: one category tracks your profit and the other your equity. The profits-based chart of accounts produces your P&L statement (revenue minus expenses). The equity-based chart of accounts produces your balance sheet, which tracks your net worth (assets minus liabilities). For our purposes I am only going to cover the P&L side but the principles are the same for both.

There are six guiding principles in this area:

1. Have the correct account grouping.
2. Separate your profit centers (and direct costs accordingly).
3. Be consistent.
4. Keep it simple.
5. Have the proper numbering system.
6. Have definitions for each account.

With regard to the grouping, put the accounts into categories that make sense.

In the Income statement they are:

- Revenue or Sales.
- Direct Costs (job costs including labor).
- Overhead Expenses (your business costs).
- Net Profit.

There are subcategories to these four sections, but these are the main ones. Separate out all your profit centers and direct expenses. By profit centers I mean the various types of work you do that create a profit for the company. Let's say you perform three different types of work, landscape maintenance, irrigation and snow plowing. You might wonder if you should separate all of them. The answer is to follow "the rule of 10". If a profit center is equal to at least 10 percent or more of your annual revenue, then it should be tracked separately (see the chapter "The Rule of 10" for a more detailed explanation)

When I was in business and my company approached $1 million in annual sales, I didn't know about the 10 percent rule. We tracked the sales of each profit center separately but not the direct costs. When we began tracking the direct costs separately for each of the three departments we discovered we were not pricing the landscape construction work high enough. We then saw clearly that our maintenance department profits had been subsidizing our construction department! If only I had learned the rule of 10 sooner, I would have saved tens of thousands of dollars. Consistency is key. Once you decide on your chart of accounts leave it alone. It should take an act of congress to change it. Make sure it is accurate from the beginning. Many owners, when creating their chart of accounts make it much too detailed while others don't have the accounts numbered correctly, which may limit future expansion and usefulness of the chart.

In the Frank Ross book, *Pricing for the Green Industry,* which I consider to be the ultimate finance book for the green industry, the author goes in-depth into this subject and refers to it as "Departmental Account Code Logic." It's very easy to get this right, but it's also equally easy to get it wrong.

In Ross' book you will find a master chart of accounts created for landscape companies that should cover all you need. In the back of the publication there are definitions that will also be helpful in understanding each of the accounts. This publication can be purchased by calling the Professional Landcare Association (PLANET) office or ordering it online from their Web site. And, if you are not a member of the association, you without question should be. When you call, join. Ross' book is only one of the many valuable educational tools they offer. When I joined in 1990 it changed me and my company.

With the knowledge of how to build the proper chart of accounts you are now on your way to gaining control of the finances in your business.

TAKE ACTION:

- If you are not tracking your sales and expenses with a P&L and a well thought out chart of accounts, consider doing so immediately.

- If you are using a P&L with chart of accounts, make sure you are tracking your profit centers separately if they are a substantial part of the total sales.

- Purchase the book, *Pricing for the Green Industry* by Frank Ross from PLANET and use it as a future accounting guide.

CHAPTER 7

Pricing – Critical to Your Success

Proper pricing is a mystery to most owners. Failing to understand how to price work properly is one of the major reasons start up businesses don't make it. Pricing is critical to the success of the company. New business owners are afraid to charge what they need, thinking "I can't charge that much. They will never accept the job." Wrong.

More than half of the landscape companies in the United States don't last five years and most are out of business before 10 years simply because they don't charge enough money to earn a profit. Most try to charge a "competitive" rate for their labor. But what if the competitors they are copying are going out of business themselves because they don't charge enough for their work? Others don't mark up job materials or don't mark them up enough. With such a mindset the more planting and construction-type work they do, and the larger they become, the more money they lose. The end result is a cash crunch and another company out of business. The sad thing is that many don't understand what happened until it's too late; others don't understand what

happened even after their business goes under.

"I didn't know what I didn't know" about pricing until my ignorance caused me to be bamboozled by one of the best. In the early years of my business we did mostly maintenance work. Any plantings were small jobs for our own customers. When we did planting work for a customer I would charge them my hourly rate for labor. All materials were charged at the same price they would have paid at a garden center. I was buying at a discount and charging retail. My discount from the garden center was generally 15 percent, so that's all I was making. I really wasn't making any money, but my overhead was low and I was learning.

One day we got a call from a property manager with a lead on a large planting job in a nearby town. I took a look at it right away and thought, "What a great job this would be to get." It was a much larger project than we had ever done before. Even better it would be done over a three-year period, so it would be steady work, too.

We received the thick bid package where we were asked to fill in "unit" pricing on a multitude of shrubs and trees. The list included large trees (4- to 5-inch cal.) to the smallest shrubs, (2 gal. in pots) from sod by the square foot, to paver stones for the walkways. We carefully calculated all the unit pricing based on our past experience.

Shortly after we sent in our proposal they asked for a meeting at their prestigious offices in New York City. We were excited. In the meeting it was explained that our pricing was OK for the larger material, but they asked us to go back and recalculate our pricing for the small and mid-sized plants and trees. After all, they reasoned, this was a big job and a lot of work "for you guys."

After the meeting we asked ourselves how our prices could be too high. But we really wanted the job"and decided to shave our bid. Our plan was to buy plants with volume discounts and make up the difference with the profit from the large trees and shrubs. It seemed to make sense at the time.

Were we ever wrong! After we submitted the new pricing and signed the contract, we began the job only to find out three months later they were no longer going to install the large trees and plants. As a matter of fact, they never had any intention of doing so. And what about the volume plant discounts? It turned out we were never able to buy enough quantity at any one time to earn a discount. We were stuck. For three years we planted and planted and planted without really making any money, an expensive education.

There was a saving grace, however. Because we lived up to the terms of the contract and did a quality job, the owner of this large construction company gave us a profitable cream puff job on his own property. He spent more than a million dollars with us during the next three years and we made up a considerable amount of the money we lost on his construction project.

I learned several lessons from this experience, but the most important was to make sure my pricing was correct whether planting small material or large or no material at all. It was at that point I realized I needed to bring in consultant to help me get my financial house in order.

TAKE ACTION:

- Properly price each of your profit centers.

- Be sure your markups for labor and materials make your company money.

- Base your pricing on your actual overhead and desired profit and not "what everyone else charges."

CHAPTER 8

Pricing – Be Accurate & Consistent

Covering the details and processes of pricing requires a book in itself, so I want to keep this as simple as possible. Here are three questions to think about.

1. Is it OK to price jobs using a multiplier?
2. Are vehicles and equipment part of direct cost or overhead?
3. How much profit should I charge?

Many contractors when pricing work with "live goods" use a simple multiplier. For example, if 10 trees cost $100 per tree wholesale, they would multiply 10 x $100 to equal $1,000. Next they would use a multiplier. Many use 2.5 times the cost, so in this case 2.5 times $1,000 equals $2,500. This would be the price they would charge the customer for the trees. The 2.5 multiplier (markup) would cover their labor, equipment, overhead and profit.

This is not an accurate way of determining your prices. If the same size trees, but a different species, cost $150 instead of $100, then the pricing at a 2.5 times markup would be too high. Here's why. The same sized tree, whether it costs $100 or $150, requires the same time to pick up, handle and install. So be careful. It is better to figure each job by the amount of time it will take rather than a uniform multiplier. Think about it, are any two jobs the same?

The second question is how to factor equipment into your price. Should you figure it separately and calculate the hours used on each job, or calculate it as part of the overall company overhead? I find that most companies include the smaller equipment in their overhead costs; the larger pieces they charge out by the hour. Having said that, I also know that one of the largest and most profitable landscape companies in the country prices every piece of equipment separately, by the hour.

In another chapter I refer to the "10 Percent Rule." That principle applies to estimating. If more than 10 percent of your total sales is spent on equipment, you probably should be charging for your equipment by the hour and not including it as an overhead expense. But remember, every company is different, some include all air-cooled engine equipment in their overhead while all other equipment is charged to the job. Go with whatever you feel comfortable as there is no right or wrong. The real key is - BE CONSISTENT.

Lastly, how much profit should you charge? My answer to this is, as much as you can! There are many factors to consider however, such as your competition, expertise in salesmanship and reputation. The key is to know "how much profit you MUST charge. You must establish a minimum profit margin in order to maintain a healthy vibrant company.

If there is one area of your company in which you can lose money fast, it's in your estimating and pricing process. Be as accurate as you can. Fax or email plant lists to vendors when you are preparing an estimate to get current pricing, and avoid unpleasant surprises. Don't assume the prices are always the same, some nurseries change based on availability and other factors. Track the labor time it takes to perform each task, keep a record and build your own labor matrix. Carefully calculate the cost of all your equipment so you have an accurate hourly rate or overhead markup for each piece. An example of some of these costs would be interest, maintenance, insurance, fuel, property taxes, etc. Be sure your estimating and pricing process is simple, accurate and consistent. This way you will take the guesswork out of this important function.

TAKE ACTION:

- Price all jobs by the hour and not with a multiplier.

- Be consistent in your pricing.

- Know the minimum profit your company needs to charge, but charge as much profit as you can.

CHAPTER 9

Pricing – Your Markup Options

There is no mystery to pricing. There are four basic ways to price work:

1. Markup the materials.
2. Markup all direct costs.
3. Markup labor and burden.
4. Markup both labor and materials.

Note that the key word in all the above is "markup." It is standard business practice to add to the cost of the materials used on a job. Why not just give materials to the customer at the same price you paid? After all, you are getting paid for your labor. The answer is that there is time and cost involved in finding and buying materials, shipping them, storing them, servicing them, replacing them if they are damaged or stolen, maintaining an inventory and most important, for the overhead, the cost of doing business. You need to earn a profit and balanced markups on labor and materials are the way to accomplish this.

Most startup landscape companies mark up their labor based on what the competition charges with very little markups for their materials. For ex-ample, if a plant sells for $20.00 retail in a garden center and they receive a 15% discount on the material, they pay $17.00 plus tax, they will charge the customer $20.00 plus tax or the retail price the customer would have paid if they purchased it in the garden center.

This method works in the beginning when the jobs are heavy with labor, but once the jobs are material intensive they will lose money because they fail to markup the materials properly. That's why so many companies do well in the beginning when they are small, but when they grow and begin to do work that involves a larger amount of materials they lose money even though their sales have increased dramatically.

The markup on labor and materials is called the dual overhead recovery method. This method creates a balance of overhead markup regardless of how much or how little material or labor is used on a job.

Proper pricing is a study in itself, so I suggest you refer to Frank Ross's book, *Pricing for the Green Industry.* Ross explains the differences and benefits of all of the four pricing methods and how to use each. The important point here is to make sure you understand the markup method you decide to use. The profitability of your business depends on it. Understanding how to price eliminates the temptation to lower your price and lose money when a customer decides to show you a competitor's lower price. Or, at least if you decide to meet your competitor's number you will be totally aware of what you are doing and it won't be an emotional decision. Become a realist. If your competitors wants to lose money that's their business, let them. Your objective is to make money. Smart pricing is the only way to do that.

There are two exceptions to the above scenario. First, make sure the competitor's lower bid is apples-to-apples with your own. Usually it is not. If that is the case, point out the differences to your prospective customer. If you are delivering more, it will cost more. Second, sometimes when we see a competitor's prices we wonder how they can work for that amount. Usually it's because they don't know how to price, or they made a mistake on their bid. But it might be because they have learned how to work more efficiently, have more skilled people, better equipment or lower company overhead. Be careful; watch your competitors. Never be complacent about your costs or productivity. Keep alert to faster, more efficient ways of doing jobs. If you are the first to discover a new or better process at less cost, you have gained an important competitive advantage. At that point you have a choice: reduce your markups or keep them the same and enjoy the profits.

TAKE ACTION:

- Get the publication *Pricing in the Green Industry* and learn how to price and markup properly.

- Be sure there is proper balance between your labor and material markups, so you will make money whether doing a job with all labor or a blend of labor and materials.

CHAPTER 10

Estimating 101

S ome believe that estimating is more of an art than a science. In my opinion, I think it's safer to view estimating as being 66 percent science and 33 percent art. The more science used in estimating the better the results. A simple way to achieve this is to create an estimating matrix or form. The matrix can be made into a printed pad or electronic form integrated into an application. One thing is for sure; by using a more formal process no items will be left out. As your company grows and expands, use of a form conditions estimators to prepare estimates in the same way and with the same rigor and process. This sounds so basic but most companies I visit have no established process for estimating. Many write the estimates on note pads and "stick them in the file." Remember, the goal is to be consistent and keep it as simple as you can.

Recently I acted as the broker in the sale of a landscape contractor's business. He had been in business for a number of years with annual sales close to seven figures. Prospective buyers require details about a business before they arrive at a purchasing decision. That means I too have to understand every aspect of the business to help close the deal. When the subject of estimating came up I asked the owner for his estimate forms. He responded, "Estimate forms?" Needless to say he didn't have any. He'd kept no records of how he arrived at his job prices! Not good.

Although this happens in many companies, it is a poor business practice. Estimating on the fly leads to pricing inconsistency. You want good, consistent estimates which will make selling jobs easier and lead to profitability on every job sold. With inaccurate or inconsistent estimates you can't compare your actual costs against your budgeted costs. What worked in my company was the creation of a simple matrix using Microsoft Excel. Each of our four estimators used the same program on their computers to make estimating simple and consistent.

Once your method is established, the next most important thing to do is establish thresholds. The larger the job the more intense scrutiny it must be given. For example, when you have relatively large jobs, I suggest having more than one estimator look at it and help with the estimate. In my company, one estimator alone could figure a job under $20,000, but if it was larger, then a minimum of two estimators were used. Jobs over $50,000 usually had two teams with two members on each team. Once we had to estimate a $1 million dollar a year maintenance job (which we won). In this case we had two teams of three, plus we used the crew su-pervisors to view the work as well. The teams worked independently, then sat down and compared notes. This process helped to eliminate the guesswork. We also visited large jobs two or three times. I used to tell my people that each time you see a big job site it shrinks. They'd laugh, but it is true. The more you see a job the more comfortable you become with it, and the smaller and more manageable it begins to look.

TAKE ACTION:

- Create an estimating matrix or form for all estimators to use.

- Keep your system simple and be consistent in its use.

- Consider a team approach when bidding larger jobs.

CHAPTER 11

Job Costing is Not an Option!

There are various ways to monitor the profitability of your business. Many owners use the income statement or the profit and loss statement (P&L). This method keeps score of how the company is doing financially, usually by the month, but this is not the same as job costing because it does not track individual job performance. When I first began job costing, or "cost tracking," I was shocked to learn that my second largest job was actually losing money. Successful and highly profitable landscape companies practice job costing. My definition of job costing is "tracking the direct cost on jobs as they are performed until they are completed, and comparing the actual data (hours, equipment and materials) to the budget estimate."

Why is job costing important? So you can track production and cost against budget to ensure that every job is on target. If the hours go over budget on some of your jobs you have the opportunity to take immediate action to correct the problem. This will also help in your estimating. If you find that you are over or under estimating jobs you will be able to make the adjustments before too much damage is done.

Company sales are made up of many individual jobs. If these jobs are bid and priced correctly and performed on budget, the gross margin for the company should be good and the company should be profitable. The objective is to keep the jobs on budget. That's where job costing comes in.

Job costing can be done manually or by computer. There are some large companies, on the order of $5 million in annual sales, that still do job costing manually, but most companies now use computers. The important thing is accuracy and timeliness of information. The faster you can get the information the sooner you can react to a problem.

If you don't have large jobs you may be thinking that job costing doesn't apply to you, but it does. If you have many small maintenance jobs, it may be very difficult to track every job; however, you could job cost them collectively. I know a number of companies that have hundreds of small residential customers. What some of them do is job cost them collectively. They track all the jobs by crew, by the day. They know exactly what a crew should be producing on an hourly, daily and weekly basis by comparing these numbers to their estimates and past performance numbers. By running their company "by the numbers", it's hard not to achieve their budgeted gross margins.

I am surprised at how many companies in our industry don't job cost. Regardless of your company size, big or small, if you don't have a job costing system it is time you think about implementing one.

In my first few years in business I was very conscious of job costing. I would add up the sales each day and divide by the total hours to see how much I was generating per hour and if that matched my estimate. My sales goal was $100 per day for my helper and myself. Believe it or not, in 1971 this was pretty good income for a residential landscape contractor. Since I did all the estimating, pricing and work, I had a pretty good handle on the profitability of all the jobs.

As time passed I moved into the commercial markets with a goal of adding one crew per year. Within a few years I was so busy with operations I could no longer effectively job cost as I had been. Luckily, I hired a consultant who discovered that my second largest job "was a dog." I realized the necessity of tracking the profitability of each and every job. I knew what I needed to do but didn't know how to accomplish it. We began the task manually (at the time no off the shelf computer software was available to

do this). Our method as cumbersome but nevertheless helpful. By the end of the 1980's, I purchased a software package that automated the general ledger for our accounting and with this new software began to create a more formal job costing system.

Labor is usually a contractor's largest expense depending on the type of work. Therefore the cost and efficiency of labor is the most important thing in the landscape business. Labor hours must be tracked on a regular basis against labor estimates.

Most companies, if they have a job cost system, look at the expended labor by the month. One company I worked with tracked hours daily by department. This may seem a bit extreme, but they were on top of their game and were very profitable. The important thing is that your system gives you the information needed so you know if you are on or off budget. You need to keep score, and tracking all labor hours for each job is a must.

One particular area to watch closely is non-billable (non-productive hours, shop time, yard time, etc.) hours. Be careful not to set up your job cost system to track only "job hours." It's best to have it include all hours – travel time, load and unload time, etc.

Many smaller contractors don't do job costing because they feel it requires expensive computer software, will cost too much to perform, or they don't have anyone to do it. Again, what you do depends on your goals and aspirations. If you want to grow and be profitable, tracking labor hours and expenses on each job is the only way to go. Don't "reinvent the wheel." There are a number of software programs to track job hours and perform complete job costing on the market with new and better ones coming out every day. Search them out, talk to other contractors, your accountant and read the trade journals.

There is a further benefit of a good system. Many of my new clients ask about setting up incentive systems to reward their people for greater productivity. I really believe in this because what you reward is what you get and if you reward efficiency that's what you will get. Many of my new clients have no job cost systems. So the first thing we have to do is put one in place. Once this is accomplished it gives them the ability to set up a system that will not only track jobs, but will make the crews "time conscious." Once the crews are rewarded for "hours saved" your jobs and company will become more profitable.

TAKE ACTION:

- Research a software package to track at least your labor hours by job.

- Using your system, carefully watch all "non-billable" hours.

- Consider offering an incentive program based on "hours saved under the estimate" once the system is set up.

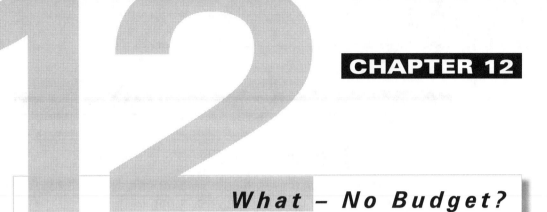

CHAPTER 12

What – No Budget?

To accurately manage your company a budget is required. A budget is really nothing more than a financial forecast or plan. Budgets are like diets: no one likes them but most of us need them. Most business owners think budgets are a mystery, something that "the big guys" do, but they don't need. I am not going to kid you; it takes quite a bit of work putting together a good budget and maintaining it. Budgets are like exercise: you hate to start and you don't know when you have the time to do it. Once accomplished however, you don't know how you lived without it. Owners have a love-hate relationship with budgets.

When I owned my landscaping company I didn't necessarily enjoy the budget planning process, but I hated the uncertainty of flying blind even more. For me creating a budget took away much of the uncertainty for the coming 12 months. The more planning and reviewing I did, the more confident and less worried I was.

Having a budget takes a lot of the gamble out of your operation because you can begin to watch and measure the performance of your company on a monthly basis. This allows you to guide your company and quickly spot problems and react if necessary. A budget lets you run your company instead of letting it running you.

If you don't know how to create a budget or just don't have the time, bring in a professional to get you started. I did, and many other smart company owners have done so as well.

TAKE ACTION:

- Create a financial budget for the next 12 months.

- At the end of each month compare budget to actual so you know the direction of your company.

- If you don't know how to create a budget, bring someone in to help.

CHAPTER 13

Invoice 'Em Early

How would you like to invoice your maintenance customers and have them pay in advance before doing the work each month? "Never happen," you say. Not true. In one of the largest maintenance contracts I ever signed I asked to be paid on the third of the month prior to the commencement of work. Notice I said "paid," not just billed! We submitted our bill electronically on the first day of every month and our money was electronically deposited into our checking account promptly on the third. That was sweet. You can do this, too. You just have to ask. It's all a matter of negotiation.

Some landscape maintenance companies begin a seasonal contract by billing their customer at the end of the first month of service. With 30-day terms, most customers will take at least that much time to pay. Corporate and commercial customers usually take even longer. In the meantime you are waiting between 60 and 75 days for your money. Let's say your sales are $1 million a year. This means that if all of your customers are billed the same way, your accounts receivable could be more than

$200,000 before you see a dime of cash! Wait a minute – financing your customers like this costs you money because you have to carry the cost of borrowing $200,000 on a line of credit to pay your people, suppliers and overhead on time. Even if you are using your own cash it doesn't make sense because it's one, tying up your money and secondly you are losing interest on the money. Some owners lend money to their company and collect interest, but this lowers the company's profit. If this is your current billing policy I would seriously consider changing it.

One commercial landscape maintenance company I worked with billed most of its customers in February, one month in advance of even setting foot on their customers' property. I asked the owner how in the world he pulled that off. He looked at me, laughed and said, "I just tell every new account that this is our policy, and they pay it". He added, "It's simply a matter of negotiation." What I realized from him and from my own experience is that the commercial customer is more concerned with the total cost per year and staying within his budget than he is with cash flow. So, take advantage of that and get your money up front.

The residential customer is different. They generally will not pay you up front, but there are various billing methods possible. Most landscape contrators invoice their customers at the end of each month based on exactly what was done. I don't like this method because of the delayed billing. In my company, we estimated all the services, arrived at a total and spread the payment out over the months of service. In the New England states, service usually begins during the middle of March, so we sent out our bills on March 1st. The amount of lawn mowings in the contract were minimums. If we exceeded the cuts we billed extra at the end of the season. This worked for us.

Other residential contractors in the snow belt bill equal "fixed" payments for basic services from May through October and bill separately for spring cleanup, mulching and fall cleanup based on the materials and hours used. This is a blend of the two methods. However you decide to do it, try and regulate your cash flow and keep it as simple as possible.

In my opinion another area where both residential and commercial contractors fall short is their billing for additional work. Most contractors wait until the end of the month to bill extra work. The additional work is added to the customer's regular monthly invoice. But this can tie up a considerable amount of cash. In my former company we decided if the work was over $500 we would send a separate invoice out the same week the work was done. We got our money in faster, our account managers were not burdened with the task of doing all the billing at the end of each month, and we never heard a peep from our clients. Everyone was happy, especially me, because we collected a few hundred thousand dollars a month weeks earlier than before we started this system. Remember - cash is still king!

TAKE ACTION:

- Negotiate "up front" payments with all your new customers, so you are always working with their money and not yours.

- Consider invoicing your customers at the beginning of the month and not the end.

- Invoice additional work at the end of each job instead of the end of each month.

CHAPTER 14

Train Them to Pay – On Time!

When I was in business I used many subcontractors. One of my best had a bookkeeper who would call my bookkeeper on the 29th day of each mont, if we owed them money, with the same question: "Are you are putting your check in the mail today?" If we ever missed a date she would call and say, "We haven't received a check as agreed, is it in the mail?"

If our check was not actually in the mail, this lady would remind my bookkeeper in a sharp, but business-like manner that they had extended us credit based on the agreed terms. Oh, she was always very pleasant and you couldn't really get angry with her, but she really held our proverbial "feet to the fire." Believe me it was painful enough to the point that my bookkeeper always paid that subcontractor first. Boy, did I wish I had this lady collecting my company's receivables!

This is the model I think we should all follow, so my cry is, COLLECT THE MONEY. Don't be embarrassed; it is your money, so collect it. You know the expression that "cash is king," without cash your company cannot function. Lack of cash is the biggest single reason for companies going bankrupt.

If you are in the landscape maintenance business, you bill your customers on a monthly basis and thus have accounts receivable. Accounts receivable refers to the money outstanding that your customers owe you. There are various payment terms that contractors can give their customers. Some put on their invoices, "Due upon receipt," or "Terms: Net 30 days." What ever your terms, the most important thing is to make them crystal clear, so your customer understands and agrees.

If a customer tries to take advantage of the terms, it is important that you enforce them without delay. Be firm. When I consult with a client, one of the first things I ask about is their accounts receivable aging. How much money is overdue 30 days, 60 days or 90 days? At times I am shocked at the amount that is overdue. If your money "gets old," it may come to the point where you have to threaten to stop service, and that can get really messy. Nip this problem in the bud. Better yet, don't ever let it get to that point in the first place. Start calling your customer as soon as the terms of the contract are exceeded.

With regard to your accounts payable (the money owed to your vendors) my thought is to pay as agreed. Never pay early and never late. If your vendors offer a discount, and some offer generous ones for prepayment or early payment, take advantage of the discount if you can. My last adviceis if you can't pay your vendor as agreed, CALL THEM and explain. Don't just disregard the invoice. If it's a lot of money, and there is a serious problem; go see them in person. Explain the problem and what your repayment plan is. If you do, they will respect you and continue to trust you. Most of them have been in the same situation at one time or another. When they ask when you are going to pay, tell them the truth even if it's not what they want to hear.

TAKE ACTION:

- Track who owes you money (from accounts receivable aging).

- Call customers as soon as they exceed your payment terms.

- Get your customers to promise when they will send their check and "hold their feet to the fire".

- Be persistent. It's your money; collect it.

- If you owe vendors money and can't pay them to meet terms, call them to arrange new terms.

CHAPTER 15

Better Have Good Contracts

In business making money is one task; keeping it is another. If you make money someone will always be there trying to take it from you.

One way to keep more money is with good contracts. During the 30 years I was in the landscaping business I only sued one customer, and could do that only because we had a solid contract in place. We had been awarded a one-year maintenance contract for a medium-sized condominium complex. After just a few months into the season grubs turned some areas brown. Some unit owners were upset, but not as upset as the president of the board of directors. A board meeting was called and we were asked to attend, but the president did not. At the meeting we explained we were not aware there had been such a serious problem the previous year and that we had applied the proper chemicals to kill these pests according to the specifications of our contract. What was supposed to be done had been done.

I told the Board that because I valued my reputation I would immediately remove the dead grass and re-sod all of the affected areas at my own expense even though I felt I had done nothing wrong. To my surprise they turned the offer down and said that they were immediately terminating our contract. I was shocked. This had never happened before. There was quite a substantial amount of money owed to us, and I felt we needed to resolve this issue. In light of the repair work I volunteered to do and their mood, I offered to settle for half of the amount owed. Before the meeting was adjourned they formally accepted my offer, and we exited the meeting cordially.

The next day the board president called and said he was not in favor of the settlement and wanted to cut the offer in half again. I told him that was not acceptable. He remained firm. I explained that he was already in violation of our contract by not giving us notice of the problem and not allowing us to correct it. He said he didn't care what the contract said, he was not changing his position and that was his final offer. If that was the case, I responded, we would let a judge decide what was fair.

I filed suit for the first time against a client. Upon the advice of my attorney we asked not only for the money owed but for the balance of the value of the contract. It took two years to come to trial. There were two half-day sessions, two weeks apart. After one month my attorney finally called to tell me the judge had decided in our favor and had given us the full amount of the suit. Ironically, the judgment was six times the amount of their offer to me.

When I heard the decision from the judge that day I was one happy guy. I was especially pleased that we had taken the time to craft a great contract. I urge you to do the same. You might think that this could never happen to you, but it's best to think of the worst. In business, the worst can and will happen.

Some of you reading this might think you don't need contracts because you only do only residential work. But let me ask you, what happens when one day you decide you want to sell your business? Or, you get a call from a competitor wanting to buy it. If you have no contracts, it is difficult to prove to your potential buyers that you have something of value to sell. Some of my clients have sent a letter to each of their customers setting out the price, the terms and specifications, etc. If they were existing customers, they weren't required to sign and return anything because once work under the terms of the letter agreement, the contract was in force. Check with your attorney to determine if this holds true in your state. With new customers a more formal agreement (contract) should

be made. Ask for a signature, and don't begin work until the executed copy is received.

You should also have contracts with all of your subcontractors. If these subs work on a number of your jobs, then have your attorney craft a "master contract agreement" and issue purchase orders (PO's) for each of their jobs as addendums to this master agreement. In this way you are always covered with a minimum amount of paperwork.

I learned how important this is the hard way because I lost a huge job to a competitor and my subs went to work for him. If I had had the non-compete in place, I could have prevented them from working for "the other team" and I never would have lost the job. From that day forward I had all of my subs sign the non-compete. What they signed said that even if I lost the job they couldn't bid on or work on the property for a period of two years. I hired a large law firm make sure this was completely enforceable.

Decide what terms you want to include in your contract, but be sure they are reasonable. Lastly, be sure to include non-compete provisions in the contract so they can't hire any of your people while working for you. This is a bit more difficult to enforce, but put it in anyway.

I also recommend having your people sign a non-compete contract. In today's competitive world it's a good idea. This is a touchy subject with many owners and their people but the subject does need to be addressed. Many times employers don't require non-competes until a trusted employee goes out and starts their own business with their former employer's customers. Happens every day. Employee non-competes are generally considered unenforceable. This might be the case, but I know few people who want to begin their business fighting a law suit, enforceable or not, because they generally don't have the money, time or desire to fight. It's one thing for them to leave and join a competitor and another for them to leave and try to begin their new business with your customers.

My final advice on contracts is to use your own contract whenever possible. If you do work for other contractors, especially if it's for new construction, they will want to have you use their contract. If they won't budge, my advice is to send their contract to your attorney.

I remember one occasion where a large construction company from a different state asked me to bid on the landscape for a building they were constructing. They sent me a four-page, fine-print contract. I sent it to my attorney. After reading it he told me if I signed it "as is" they basically didn't have to pay me if they didn't feel like it. I had absolutely no recourse, period. Needless to say we redlined many of their provisions set forth in their contract. They yelled and screamed a bit and said we couldn't do that, "bla bla bla." But shortly thereafter sent it back signed with all our changes.

Don't be intimidated. Don't think you won't get the job because you cross out some of the provisions in a preprinted agreement. If you disagree with the provisions, cross them out. Contractors negotiate various provisions all the time. Read all contracts carefully. Have your attorney review and explain the terms and conditions until you understand them. And, for heaven's sake get a great contract attorney who is familiar with the contracts in your business and has the ability to negotiate when needed.

In summary, you need a number of contracts. Consider having one for your maintenance work, one for landscape construction work, one for your subcontractors, and a non-compete for your key people.

TAKE ACTION:

- Work with an attorney to craft a contract that offers a fair but specific remedy if the customer decides not to pay their bill.

- Have a specific contract for landscape maintenance, construction and snow. Different types of work require different contracts.

- Have contracts with all your subcontractors. Include non-competes in them.

- Have your contract include an indemnification clause to relieve you of their liability.

- Have all your "key" people sign non-compete agreements when they are hired.

- Don't ever, ever, ever sign a contract without having your attorney review it first, period!

CHAPTER 16

Money – Checks & Controls

A few years ago my associate and I gave a presentation to landscape contractors at a state association meeting. We spoke on sales and marketing. After our talk a very successful company owner took us to dinner at one of the finest restaurants in the city. It was a great night. However, our conversation that evening eventually turned toward a negative situation he had recently experienced. He explained how his bookkeeper who had been with him for some 10 years, had embezzled hundreds of thousands of dollars from the company. He explained that she had set up fake companies and wrote checks to these companies for years, forging his signature.

She was very careful in the amount and timing of the "bogus" invoices she submitted. He finally accidentally discovered what she was doing while she was on vacation. How did she get away with this for so long? Simple. When the cancelled checks came from the bank she opened the envelope; no one else ever saw them. He said he pressed charges, and she was serving quite a long sentence in state prison.

He asked who opened my check statements. I told him my bookkeeper did. Right then and there he advised me to have these envelopes sent directly to me for opening. I took his advice to heart. I didn't always go through every check each month, but from then on I opened the envelope from the bank and every few months went through every one. Who opens the envelope with cancelled checks at your business?

Another area requiring control is credit cards. Some companies give their drivers major oil company credit cards, i.e. Shell, Mobil, etc. For the most part people are honest, but there are exceptions.

One of my clients told me this cautionary tale. One of the major fuel companies called him with a concern. The fuel company's security had found a charge for $175 for gasoline for one truck. He checked it out and found that there had been a $35 purchase for gas and the balance were lottery tickets. My suggestion to prevent this from happening is to use a gasoline credit card service that tracks purchase details. Their monthly reports will provide you with an individual report by vehicle. The report includes the vehicle registration number, mileage, date, time of day the sale occured and amount of fuel used. In some cases a discount is earned once a certain volume of gas is purchased. One card many landscape companies use is Wright Express. There are others and I suggest checking them out. These cards can be used at almost all gas stations anywhere in the country.

The last area I want to cover is company credit cards given to employees. In some cases companies obtain corporate credit cards for their people. The company expects that only business expenses be charged on this card. Each card can have its own limit based on the needs of the card holder. This system works pretty well because if the expense reports are not turned in by the card holder the card will not be paid by the company and the card company will automatically place their card on hold. However, this rarely happens because the card holders credit will be adversely effected - so they are generally quite prompt in turning in receipts so the cards are paid on time. Make it a firm policy that corporate issued cards are never to be used for personal use. Ask your people to give you a detailed accounting each month for all expenses. Check with the various credit card companies because there are a number of different programs they offer in this regard.

TAKE ACTION:

- Open your monthly bank statement and review the cancelled checks. Note: most banks are no longer sending cancelled checks so you can now see your account electronically by going on line.

- Consider using an independent company for your fuel purchases that can track all the details of every transaction by vehicle.

- Have credit cards in your peoples names and insist on an accounting for all company credit cards or the bills will not be paid and their card will be place on hold.

PART 3

Your People

Chapter   1   Finding Good People   89

Chapter   2   Hire Right!   93

Chapter   3   Your New Employee's First Day   95

Chapter   4   Company Culture & Team Balance   99

Chapter   5   Your People Plan   101

Chapter   6   Develop a Learning Organization   103

Chapter   7   Retain Valuable People   107

Chapter   8   Compensation   111

Chapter   9   Job Descriptions   113

Chapter 10   HR Policies & Handbooks   115

Chapter 11   Your Office Staff   117

Chapter 12   Managing Supervisors   119

Chapter 13   Taking Chances on People   121

Chapter 14   Coaching & Mentoring   123

CHAPTER 1

Finding Good People

The greatest challenge in the landscape industry is finding and retaining good people. For that simple reason, recruiting must to be done on a continuous basis. I always considered finding the best people for my company one of the most important things I could do as an owner. Ask yourself this: Would you work for your company? It's important to know why or why not.

When you are starting out, you will attract people to work for you because they need jobs. You will have to pay a competitive wage, but the real secret to keeping people in the early years is to treat them well. If you pay fairly, treat your people with respect and do what you promise to do, most of your people will stay with your company long-term.

As your business grows, the best source of quality future employees is your workforce. Spread the word among your people and offer a reward for referrals that results in valuable new hires. Companies across the country offer rewards from $100 to $300. Most companies pay the reward after the new hires prove themselves and stay for a certain period of time, say 60 or 90 days. Usually, these new workers prove valuable because your employees won't want to ruin their reputations by referring people that will reflect badly on them. After all, they want to keep their jobs, too.

As a business owner, I was always looking for people. I remember stopping at a donut shop for coffee. When I went in, I noticed a young man in the parking lot working hard picking up papers and sweeping the lot. When I came out, he was still hard at work. I engaged him in a conversation, gave him my card and told him if he ever wanted to work in landscaping to give me a call. He called the next day. He worked for me for quite some time before deciding to go back to school.

On another occasion, I went to retail garden center to pick up six flats of annuals. After paying for them, a clean-cut young man came out with the first flat. When he saw I was in a car and not a truck, he got newspaper to cover the seats. I liked his friendly accommodating attitude, and told him if he ever wanted to consider working in a landscaping business to give me a call.

I didn't want to be unprofessional and steal help from the garden center so I simply planted the idea in his head. I suggested he call if he was interested in a different type of job. He did call and I hired him. Not only did he work for me, but he also recruited his two brothers. All three continued to work for me until they graduated from college.

I have noticed that the "help" problem depends on a company's geographic location. Some companies have no problem finding good people to fill their crews, while others have a really tough time. The Federal H-2B program has helped many companies. This program allows workers to come to the United States to work on a temporary basis. I used the H-2B program with great success.

If you are interested in this program, my advice is to contact a labor agency like Amigos Labor Solutions in Dallas, Texas. Agencies like these specialize in the program and can help simplify the process. Also, consult with industry peers who use the H-2B program. They can offer valuable insight from a "been there, done that" perspective.

As your company grows, you will need knowledgeable people to sell the work and manage the crews. It may be difficult in the beginning because career-minded people want to learn and grow. The challenge for you is to provide this opportunity for them. Again, ask yourself the question: Why would they work for you?

If you have trouble finding good people for management positions, scout local colleges or vocational schools. In my business, I relied on a number of college instructors as consultants. They got to know my business. Then, once they were confident in my reputation, they referred their students to me. As your good reputation improves, talented people will be attracted to your company. Momentum will build.

It is proven that colleges are a great place to find talented people, especially designers, managers and horticulturists. The best way to work with a college is to get involved. Attend their job fairs, meet students and professors. Offer to speak when they need business people for programs.

Also, don't forget your local vocational schools or high schools with agricultural programs. These are sometimes untapped sources for workers who want to pursue full-time landscape careers.

TAKE ACTION:

- Offer a friendly work environment where employees have opportunities for advancement.

- Consider the H-2B program.

- Get involved with local colleges and schools to recruit potential managers from their student bodies.

CHAPTER 2

Hire Right!

How do you know if you hired the right person for the job? If this thought has crossed your mind, you're not alone. You can improve your odds of recruiting the right person for the job by implementing the following four processes.

First, ask the right questions and listen. There are plenty of books that explain how to interview prospective employees. One point these books will make is the importance of not talking too much. If you are talking, then you are not learning. Let the interviewee talk. Wait until the end of the interview to tell "your story."

Second, call the prospective employee's former employer or workmates and ask them questions. If they sound evasive, press for an answer to this question: Would you rehire this worker? A simple yes or no will tell the story. If the answer is no, you may reconsider hiring the person to work at your company.

Third, give interviewees personality and value tests. I suggest this only for key management positions because of the cost, but these tests are worth every penny. You may find out more than you even want to know about the candidate. But wouldn't you rather know who you are hiring before they join your company and you invest in their training? These tests are available online and generally take only 20 minutes for interviewees to complete.

Finally, invite candidates to a lunch or dinner. See how they conduct themselves in a relaxed atmosphere. Interacting with a person at different times, in different places and in different situations will help you better evaluate them.

Once we interviewed three candidates for an account manager position. It was a job that required handling more than $1 million in sales. My operations manager and I did the final interviews for each candidate over dinner. We took each one out separately, went to the same restaurant, sat at the same table and asked similar questions. Each dinner lasted about two and a half hours.

We took our time and made each candidate feel comfortable. We talked about a variety of subjects. It is amazing what you will find out about people after they relax. They talk more about themselves sharing interests, hobbies and goals. After saying good night to each candidate, we cast our ballots. Was it thumbs up or down?

The first two candidates got a thumbs down without discussion. We both agreed that the first two men talked themselves out of the job at dinner. Neither struck us as career people. We couldn't identify any love or passion for landscaping in their conversations. The last candidate, the one we were initially skeptical of, was the one that shined. He loved and had real passion for the work and wanted to make a career out of landscaping. We hired him and he served the com-

pany well for years. It was worth the time and energy to go through the longer hiring process.

I really believe in taking the time to identify people who are engaged in their work, especially salespeople and managers. Passionate people think about their work. Hire people who want to learn and improve themselves and the company. And be sure you hire people not solely based on their knowledge or where they went to school, but on their attitude and aptitude. People with positive attitudes and the ability to learn are out there. Now go find them!

TAKE ACTION:

- People with positive attitudes and the ability to learn are out there. Now go find them.

- Follow these four suggestions:
  1. Ask the right questions and listen.
  2. Make calls to past employers.
  3. Do personality/value testing where appropriate.
  4. Observe candidates in various situations, like lunches or dinners.

- Hire people with good attitudes and aptitudes.

CHAPTER 3

Your New Employee's First Day

Everyone readily admits that people make the difference in a company, and great people make companies great. Knowing that, how do you introduce new hires to your company? Consider what attitudes are formed during their first eight hours on the job. If the first day, week, and month are positive, then new hires will settle in and should develop a positive attitude about their future at the company.

Statistics show that new hires who have bad feelings about their first few days and weeks will not last. New hires may have residual job offers during that first month, and if they don't feel comfortable, they may jump ship, leaving everyone wondering, "What happened to…?"

Let's be conscious of how we treat our new hires, especially in the early days of employment. This chapter will give you some ideas so you can establish a first-day protocol that will leave a positive impression.

The following scenario is what happens at many companies. A new hire reports to work early and is told to wait awhile. After all, first thing in the morning, managers are busy dispatching crews. After an hour or more of waiting, the new hire finally meets the supervisor, who assigns the new person to a crew. The rest is history. No introductions, no greeting, no hospitality, no manners. At most companies, the treatment is not much better for new hires in management positions. How would you feel? This is shameful.

Let's replay this scenario the way it should or could be. When a new hire arrives for his first day, you should greet him properly. If you know you can't meet a new employee until crews are out the door, then suggest a later start time. Treat new hires no differently than you would a dinner guest at your home. Would you tell the guest to arrive at 6:30 p.m. and stall him for an hour while you organized dinner in the other room? Of course not!

Now, let's talk about the right way to treat new employees. Greet them properly. Introduce them to crews, management, office staff, anyone they will work with in your organization.

At this point, provide them with a history of your company. Emphasize how proud you are of the business you built. Explain their job expectations. Make sure new hires understand their roles and how their performance is important to the overall success of the company.

After this orientation, give them paperwork to complete. This paperwork might have been filled out in advance, but sharing the company history and how proud you are of the organization's accomplishments first sets the stage. Now, your new hires are ready for more than casual introductions. Bring them to the site where they will work and introduce them to their colleagues and supervisors. And before they leave that first day, it's a good idea for you or a manager to meet them and answer any questions. Ask them, "How was your day?" Let them know their hard work will be appreciated.

How do you think new hires will feel if they are treated this way? Guaranteed, they will have a good impression of you, their new supervisor, their co-workers and their new job in general.

Remember, new employees' friends and families will ask about the first day. As an employer, you want new hires to deliver a positive message to others. By giving them a great first impression, they will look forward to Day Two and a long career at your organization. The trick is to implement a system so the way new employees are treated the first day becomes policy.

A friend of mine on the West Coast owned a very successful landscape company. One thing he and his partner believed in was the importance of a great first day. To accomplish this, he developed a 30-minute video detailing the company history. In the video, he described how he and his partner started, including interviews with employees. He showed his people working on site. He was proud of what he created.

After watching the video, he discussed it with new employees before asking them to fill out paperwork. Next, they were issued uniforms and necessary safety equipment, then given a brief tour of their facility. Finally, the owner gave a short talk to new hires about his high expectations for the company and all employees.

One important point he highlighted for all new hires was how they could advance in the company. New employees saw a clear picture of how they could climb the company's career ladder if they worked hard and applied themselves. Each person was important to the company's success.

All new hires left that session feeling like they would be working for an owner who is proud of the company's roots. And that owner was clear about his values, vision and mission.

This landscape company dedicated four hours to orientation. At the end of that time, new hires were give the company manual and sent home to read it. They were paid for a full day of work.

Some would say this was a waste of money or they couldn't afford it. I believe it's an investment in the future of your company. I understand many small owners can't possibly do all of this, but my recommendation is to do whatever you can. In your own way, make your new employee's first day a great one.

TAKE ACTION:

- Make the first day a positive one for every new hire.

- Create a process where all new hires are treated with respect and learn about the company.

- Tell your story to every new hire and be sure they are aware that you value team members and their accomplishments.

- Be clear about your expectations and explain how new hires can advance in your organization.

CHAPTER 4

Company Culture & Team Balance

You have probably heard the expression, "The whole is greater than the sum of its parts." This is certainly true when people enjoy working together in a business and are focused on a common goal. There is a synergy, a positive chemistry that exists when people work well together. For this reason, it's smart to hire people with diversity in terms of personality, temperament and knowledge.

In some companies I visit, I find that many of the employees share similar personalities. They are a lot like the owner, and this makes sense. After all, the owner hired them. We all have a tendency to hire people with whom we share interests or personality traits. But when this happens, an imbalance in the company culture can occur.

For example, if the owner has an easy-going personality, he should hire an operations person with a more direct "let's get the job done" attitude. How profitable would the company be if everyone were laid back?

One successful company I am familiar with is owned by two brothers. One is an easy-going, outgoing guy; everyone loves him. He runs the sales, marketing and administrative side of the business while his brother, the perfect complement, runs operations. His brother is the proverbial whip, the guy that makes it happen, gets it done. This combination of personalities provides a great balance for the company.

The key to establishing this positive teamwork culture is regular meetings, good communication and strong leadership. When the owner or managers clue their people in on "what's going on," all employees feel they can help shape the future of the company. This knowledge, this type of communication, breeds loyalty and commitment.

When a company does not have meetings and lacks communication, people feel detached. They don't care about the company; they just work there. I have visited a number of companies where owners and managers focus on work and not their people. This is fine for a while, but once the company grows larger and employees gain more responsibility, they become frustrated with the owner. Attitudes quickly turn from positive to negative. Good people leave the company for other opportunities.

To avoid this, hold regular meetings. These are beneficial for giving the owner an opportunity to share his dreams and plans for the future. Employees want direction, but they also want to offer input. They want to feel like they are making a difference. That's why communication is key.

Engage and challenge your people. But then ask for their ideas and listen. Don't just hear what they are saying. Respond.

Treat employees fairly and show them a future in your company. Once you give them responsibility and authority, get out of the way, because they will "make it happen." This behavior builds trust, loyalty and a positive culture where everyone wants to work.

I would be remiss if I did not mention those few people who can sour the culture of a company. These are the complainers and gossipers. For them, nothing is ever right. Their glass is always half empty, and they rarely show a genuine smile. They are critical of all but their closest friends, who are in the same complainers' club.

Some call these people "destroyers." This term is appropriate because, if allowed, they can totally ruin the culture of a company. If you have these type of people in your company, show them the negative effect they have on the company and others who work there. And if they don't change after sufficient time, help them find a job in another company they feel "fits" them better.

TAKE ACTION:

- Be conscious of the balance of personalities in your company.

- Hire the right personality type for each job.

- Let your people in on "what's going on."

- Don't put up with destroyers. They will weaken your company culture.

CHAPTER 5

Your People Plan

People are the most important part of any company. Your success depends on them. In the beginning, you have to wear a lot of hats. You are the company. You perform every function, including selling jobs, estimating, buying materials and supplies, repairing and maintaining equipment, billing and often working in the field. Although those formative stages are difficult, you can gain hands-on understanding of how the business works, your strengths and what roles you enjoy the most.

In my case, I gravitated to what I enjoyed – selling, marketing, managing the operations, etc. – and let my wife and accountant focus on their strengths: the numbers. Over time I learned the numbers, but it was painful. I was aware that my success was dependent on my understanding of the financials. I will admit, however, that as soon as I could afford it, I hired experts to handle this part of the business.

Now, back to people. Once you start to grow, you will want to hire employees who are strong in areas where you are weak. As I mentioned previously, don't make the mistake of hiring people who are exactly like you. Sure, you'll feel comfortable hiring people with similar traits, but this won't help you fill needed positions in your organization. Think about what you like to do, and hire people to manage the other roles.

As my business grew to more than $1 million in sales, then $2 million and quickly $3 million, I developed what I now call a People Plan. We had an organizational chart that included every person who worked for the company. The organization chart hung on the wall in my office. Every year, I gathered my key managers and we rated every person on the chart based on their value to the company. The goal was to see whether we had the right people in the right jobs, and to identify the future needs of the company.

When I do strategic planning with a client, we put together a People Plan and organization chart that anticipates personnel needs for the upcoming three years. We also rate the existing people by department.

With this information, you can determine whether managers require additional education, if the quality of your people is spread evenly among departments, and when you will need to hire additional managers.

If your company is small, this kind of planning may be too extensive. Still, it's good to think along these terms so you can anticipate your future people needs. After all, people are your most important company asset. So it's critical to spend the time each year to evaluate them and your future needs.

TAKE ACTION:

- Create an organization chart and revise as needed.

- Make a People Plan to evaluate your current staff.

- Consider your people needs for the upcoming three years.

CHAPTER 6

Develop a Learning Organization

Too many company owners pay lip service to training, but they don't practice what they preach. Their excuses run the gamut: Training is too expensive. It takes too much time. Employees don't care anyway. We'd rather focus on making money. The list goes on. The ironic part of this thinking is if you don't educate your people, many of them will leave.

The motto these days is, "If we're not growing we're going." Employees want to grow, to learn. They believe the more they learn, the more they earn. Education helps them advance.

In fact, aside from having a smarter workforce, one of the added benefits of having a learning organization is much better employee retention. But again, the challenge is to show newly educated workers how they can advance within the company. Without a clear career path for them to follow, they may look for other opportunities.

As difficult as it is to retain valuable people these days, you don't want them to leave. But in many green industry companies, there is a 15 to 20 percent turnover. High turnover kills you, especially if you're losing managers. Losing good people can cost a company tens of thousands of dollars.

Personnel experts say the cost to replace an experienced manager is 1.5 times his or her annual salary. Plus, the employee's acquired knowledge and experience is gone forever.

The good news is your company doesn't have to be a part of this statistic. I worked with one company that had a 35 percent turnover rate. By making some needed personnel changes and creating a learning organization, that number was reduced to less than 10 percent in just a few years.

Great landscape companies provide education for their people. The result is a thirst for knowledge that permeates the organization. With this, people accept new ideas and embrace change.

When creating a learning organization, consider the special needs of your employees. What knowledge do they need to grow? For example, Hispanic workers have two big needs: to overcome the language barrier and to get drivers' licenses. Help them and they will become even more valuable assets to your company.

Some of the educational programs you will want to teach will cover technical aspects. Many of your managers are capable of teaching these seminars. Some companies have programs for learning English and Spanish. Others teach basic management skills in-house. Or, they may send people to night classes like Dale Carnegie for sales or management. There are numerous seminars held by the American Management Association on a wide variety of subjects. Enroll your managers in courses like these and watch them blossom. Also, many state business organizations provide "soft skills" training for very reasonable prices.

There are an abundance of training opportunities out there. If you don't know where to start, call your local community college, state agricultural extension, industry associations, insurance companies and manufacturers.

Another idea is to offer your own company "certification." Provide training courses that your own employees teach. Employees interested in learning can take these courses and, upon earning certification, advance within your organization or receive pay incentives.

Also, Internet training is beginning to catch on. Some of the larger companies already encourage employees to enroll in online courses. This type of education is convenient because it allows students to study at home at their own pace. Online training will become more widespread in the industry as the cost goes down and the quality improves.

It's best to have one person champion the educational process. Serious training is a business strategy that requires money and an ongoing commitment.

If setting up training programs sounds too formidable for you or your people, you could bring in green industry consulting companies to help.

To conclude, think about creating a learning organization. Make training a priority and the results will pay off well into the future.

TAKE ACTION:

- Create a learning organization.

- Assign one person to champion the training process.

- Determine your educational needs and outline a short- and long-term educational program for your people.

- Create a career path so your people know how knowledge can help them advance within the company.

- If the task is too big, hire outside professionals to assist.

CHAPTER 7

Retain Valuable People

In reflection, I believe there are seven things an owner or manager can do to keep loyal employees and keep employees loyal. Let's review them one at a time.

1. Hire people with potential.
Try to hire the person with the potential to climb the ladder. Even if you hire someone in a humble position, ask yourself if this person has the potential to become more. Always hire the candidate who has the potential to advance, regardless of the position you are trying to fill.

2. Hire career-minded individuals who love the work.
Part of the trick to retaining good people is to hire the right people to begin with. If landscaping is "just a job" to the people on your team, it will be difficult to maintain a stable, quality-minded workforce. Seek out people who love what they do. Part of the reason many large landscape companies hover around horticultural colleges is to attract students who are smart and love working outdoors or with plants. That's why they are in school. They want to make a career in the green industry. So whether they are students, former students or ambitious workers who gravitate to the outdoors, find people who love the work.

3. Pay employees well.
You can do everything else right, but if you don't pay your people well, eventually they will leave. Find out what the competition pays and offer your employees the same rate or more. The worst thing that can happen is to lose a great crew supervisor to a competitor who is willing to pay $1 per hour more. When I was in my business I got one of the best account managers ever because the company he was with promised him a truck and didn't give it to him. This man handled the greatest volume of work, was one of the nicest guys I've ever known and stayed with me until I sold the company.

4. Show workers how they can advance in your organization.
After a while, most people will get tired of what they are doing. People need change and want to be challenged. I suggest you create what is

commonly referred to in the business world as a "career ladder." We covered this concept in previous chapters.

Show the people on your team how they can advance if they apply themselves. Make it clear exactly how much more money they can make if they are willing to accept greater responsibility. Use the military as an example. A private in the Army knows if he applies himself, he can move up in ranks. There is no mystery to it. There is a clear job description, and pay rates are published. The Army also has bonuses for staying with "the company." If it weren't so dangerous, their "employees" probably would never leave.

So, copy a successful formula like the military's and publish the job descriptions and pay rates. Show your people how they can grow and make more money if they stay and accept responsibility.

5. Include key employees in your plans for the future.

Most of the companies I visit don't tell their people what's going on. Their owners don't necessarily have secrets. They just don't communicate well. I once visited a fairly prominent company where the owner told me he never held meetings. The only time the staff got together was for a summer picnic and a year-end holiday party.

Don't follow this example. Instead, involve your people, tell them about your plans and ask for their opinions and ideas. If you involve your people and they feel like they have a voice

in what's going on, they will want to stay with your organization for a long time.

6. Create a learning organization.

In order to help people climb the career ladder in your company and feel challenged, as I mentioned earlier, you need to create a learning organization. This means you must help your people learn. Invite outside speakers to your company, send employees to seminars, empower your own "internal experts" and ask them to give seminars on their expertise. Encourage all employees to work toward whatever certifications your local, state and national organizations offer. Set up training programs and really foster education.

If you do all of this, or even some of it, your employees will develop as people and professionals. In effect, you will improve the quality of your company's product, and customers will be more satisfied. Your profit margins will grow. And finally, your people will appreciate this learning culture because they will have the ability to improve their skills and will not want to leave this creative learning atmosphere.

7. Show your team appreciation, respect and trust.

You can do all six things above, but if you don't tell your people you appreciate them, show your people respect and trust them, they will not be loyal. You will lose valuable employees to the competition. However, it is important to note that money alone will not retain workers. I know of organizations that can't pay their people what they would really like to for various reasons. Yet because of the owner's sincere appreciation, respect and trust in his people, they are totally loyal to him. These qualities don't cost one penny, but they mean everything.

TAKE ACTION:

- Hire people with potential.

- Hire career-minded individuals who love the work.

- Pay your employees well.

- Show people how they can advance in your organization.

- Share your company's plans for the future.

- Create a learning organization.

- Show employees appreciation, respect and trust.

Compensation

If people are your most important asset, be sure to pay them well. As a general rule, it's best to pay your key people a little better than the competition. Also keep in mind, compensation includes salary and benefits, so you'll want to make sure the benefits are comparable or better than your competitors'.

Here's some advice concerning compensation:

- Make sure you are paying a competitive rate and there is a substantial difference between what you pay field employees and managers. There needs to be a real difference in pay between levels of responsibility, or employees won't work toward promotions.

- Rank all of your employees from most important to least. Do this every six months. Then compare their wages to ensure they are being paid according to their value. If someone is overpaid, make sure they know it and ask them to accept more responsibility. If they are not being paid enough, give them a raise.

- Don't delay in giving a deserving person a raise. Once someone's performance or value to your organization warrants a pay increase, give it to him. Don't wait. I have watched crew members become managers, but because their compensation was not adjusted promptly in their new position, they marketed their capabilities to the competition and away they went.

- Meet with your people formally every six months for a performance review. Talk to them about what they are doing right and where they can improve. Make sure they are clear as to what they need to do to be more valuable to the company and to make more money.

As the owner, you also deserve fair compensation, but take a conservative salary – no more than you would pay someone else to do your job. At the end of the year, you can take a bonus or dividend once profits have been determined.

Compensation is not the main reason people work in landscaping. Most love what they do and find great personal satisfaction in improving their environment. But, a fair compensation is necessary to live in this expensive world, so let's make sure what we pay is fair. Otherwise, we will lose our best people.

TAKE ACTION:

- Pay a competitive rate.

- Rank all of your people annually and ensure you are paying them fairly.

- Conduct performance reviews every six months.

- Don't procrastinate when giving pay increases.

CHAPTER 9

Job Descriptions

Job descriptions are just that: the basic responsibilities of a particular job. Job descriptions are important for a number of reasons, but foremost, to clarify the responsibilities of a particular job. Once descriptions are created, these also can be used in employment advertisements to help explain to job applicants what the position requires. Job descriptions also qualify people for pay raises and promotions, help establish training needs and define reasons for termination.

There should be a job description for every job in your company. The description should list separately the responsibilities and qualifications and may list physical, mental and educational requirements.

Job descriptions or positions can be broken down based on responsibility and qualifications. For example, Gardener 1, 2, 3 positions would have separate job descriptions, sets of responsibilities and pay grades. This ranking system gives people a career ladder to climb.

The Gardener 1 position would be for a new person with no landscape knowledge. As the employee gains experience and knowledge, he or she could be promoted to the Gardener 2 position, and so forth. This system encourages workers to learn so they can earn more as they climb the ladder. Most importantly, these job descriptions set a pay range for each position. That way, employees will know when to expect raises and realize that pay increases depend on their performance.

One of the best examples of how job descriptions encourage employees is the story of a friend of mine, Wayne, who came from Jamaica and worked as a carpenter's helper. The carpenter no longer needed his services, so he referred him to me. Wayne came with an excellent recommendation. Despite the fact that the young man had no education, could not read or write and had no driver's license, I hired him. It turned out to be one of the best decisions I ever made.

When I hired Wayne, my company had written job descriptions to show employees their opportunities within the company. We posted the job descriptions along with the pay grades for each position. Wayne saw these opportunities and took advantage of the winter layoff. He took reading classes at the local high school. Within a short time, he received his General Education Diploma (GED).

After that, I learned he was taking classes in writing composition. He then began studying for the State of Connecticut's Pesticide Supervisory License. This is a very difficult set of tests with two parts: a written and oral exam. College grads often fail it the first time. After a couple years with much persistence on his part, Wayne passed the State test. We were all so proud of him!

This achievement entitled Wayne to a new, higher paying position. He worked his way up the career ladder and earned a good pay raise. When I sold my company, he was the assistant operations manager. Oh, and I also want to mention that we were all invited to Wayne's wedding a few years ago. It was a memorable day for a guy who had come so far so fast.

After the occasion, I thought to myself how glad I was to have set up a system that allowed him to progress as he did. The lessons from this are clear: Job descriptions give clarity and bring opportunity to all of your employees. Be sure you take time to write them.

TAKE ACTION:

- Write job descriptions for each position in your company.

- Create a career ladder so employees understand how to advance in your organization.

- Encourage advancement by posting positions and pay ranges.

CHAPTER 10

H.R. Policies & Handbooks

As companies grow, the need for written benefits and policies becomes even more important. There are many issues that crop up while running a business, and if the owner does not have a firm policy on how to deal with these issues, it can lead to liability exposure and lawsuits often instigated by their own employees.

I suggest one of two ways to handle this. Either have a great handbook that has been reviewed by an attorney that specializes in labor law, or at the very least, create a simple list of policies so your people fully understand the company benefits. Whatever you do, don't type up a handbook and distribute it without consulting legal counsel! I know firsthand because a one-sentence mistake in my policy manual cost me $75,000.

My next piece of advice is to keep on hand an expert human resources (HR) consultant to guide you in making decisions and keep you out of trouble. One wrong hire or one wrong fire can cost you dearly! A client of mine recently settled a labor dispute with his employees to the tune of $250,000. Unfair, I think, but guess what? He had to pay it.

It is also wise to contact your insurance agent and investigate the cost of protection for various types of discrimination exposures. The cost of this insurance has become quite affordable, and it's worth every penny.

TAKE ACTION:

- If you decide to create a policy handbook, consult with an attorney who can review the manual first.

- Partner with a human resources consultant you can rely on to answer questions.

- Investigate insurance to cover potential lawsuits.

CHAPTER 11

Your Office Staff

In most new small businesses, the owner wears all the hats including managing office responsibilities. As the company grows, the new owner must decide when to hire a bookkeeper or administrative assistant, and whether to create an office for the business. Many landscapers never make this leap and end up doing all of the office work, which prevents them from growing their businesses.

In many companies, the wife or children assume administrative roles to free up the owner's time so he can concentrate on operations. This is common in small family-owned businesses, where the wife usually works in a home office. For the most part, these arrangements work out quite well, until the business outgrows the home office or family members can no longer manage finances because of the size of the business. At this point, an owner must make decisions: Is it time to move to a larger office? Should the owner hire more qualified office staff, or do nothing at all and suppress the growth of the business?

This is when an owner must decide whether to grow and expand operations, or keep it small. The choice is different for every owner.

Having the right people in your office with the proper equipment plays a huge role in the smooth operations and success of your company. Initially, many owners underestimate the importance of this. For these reasons, if you decide to hire support staff, it is important to find pleasant employees with positive personalities.

Often, owners begin by bringing in a bookkeeper to help with the needed accounting. Ideally, the bookkeeper should also serve as your assistant and handle many of the administrative functions. Because of their personalities, many bookkeepers will not want to do this, so beware.

In conclusion, be sure the office staff and equipment keep pace with the growth of the business. A great office and staff will relieve stress and allow you to oversee operations and focus on healthy growth.

TAKE ACTION:

- Don't allow your office environment to restrict your growth potential.

- Be sure the office and staff can keep peace with the growth of your operation.

- Hire efficient, pleasant workers to manage your office. Remember, this staff is often customers' first impression of your business.

CHAPTER 12

Managing Supervisors

One of the keys to success in any landscape company is the ability for the owner to properly manage supervisors. Delegating and "letting go" of the work you have managed for years is one of the hardest things for an owner.

Most owners get into trouble with their managers because they delegate responsibilities without authority, or they delegate responsibilities and micromanage every single action the manager takes. This is frustrating for managers. How would you feel if an owner asked you to perform a task and then breathed down your neck the whole time?

Before delegating authority, an owner must first establish a level of trust with managers. It's important for the owner to measure results, not individual actions. Remember, there are levels of responsibilities when delegating, and it's best to start by assigning smaller jobs. See how the manager performs, then build.

For example, delegate a small supervisory task and ask the manager to check back with you at various predetermined stages. As you grow more confident, give this manager more responsibilities and ask him to check in with you less often. Finally, once you are totally confident in his technical or managerial skills, let the manager do the job and check in with you on an as-needed basis. Keep in mind, this process may take a number of years.

A great management tool that helps set clear goals is a score card. On the left side of the card make a list of items you want to track on a single job or multiple jobs. For example, gross margin, labor as a percentage of sales, subcontractor costs, accidents, additional work sold, etc. To the right of each of these items, make three columns and title them at the top from left to right: Below Goal; Goal; Exceeded Goal. Now fill in the boxes.

This is a great tool to use to track managers' progress. As you do this, be sure to reward managers who consistently exceed goals.

TAKE ACTION:

- Agree on clear goals.

- Clarify managers' responsibilities.

- Give managers the authority to fulfill their responsibilities.

- Create time lines for accomplishing these goals.

- Conduct regular meetings to review progress and measure results.

CHAPTER 13

Taking Chances on People

Hiring smart is finding the right person for the right job. Sounds simple enough, but sometimes you're successful at this, and sometimes you're not. With practice and good interviewing skills you can improve your odds, as we discussed in Chapter Five. But sometimes, you just have to take a chance on people.

One fellow I took a chance on went by the name "Batsy." I had been in business only a few years when I hired him. A couple of weeks after his start in Spring, he walked into work at 7 a.m. with his hair soaking wet. He was 18 years old, had long blond hair past his shoulders, and that morning looked like Tarzan after going for a swim in the jungle.

I asked him why his hair was so wet. He replied, "It rained last night." I said I knew that, but no one else had come to work with wet hair. "You don't understand," he said matter-of-factly. "I slept in a tree last night." I thought he was joking, so I asked where? He said in the city park. Intrigued, I asked, "How did you manage not to fall out of it?" He said, "I tie myself in with my belt." I persisted, "Aren't you afraid someone will see you in the park?" He replied, "No. I'm up high in a maple tree with so many leaves no one can see me up there."

Yikes. I thought I'd heard them all until that story.

Then I learned that Batsy wasn't joking, and in addition to sleeping in a tree he buried his belongings so no one would steal them. Everyone who heard this story that morning was blown away. It turned out that Batsy's mother was divorced and her live-in boyfriend threw him out. Being just 18 and not having enough money to rent a place, he did the best he could. We got to work finding him a decent place to live.

We took Batsy to a boarding house not far away and advanced him money for rent. During the next couple of days, his workmates really came through for him with pots and pans, tons of canned food, and clothes. Batsy stayed with us for years and became a crew supervisor. Sometimes, it pays to take chances with people. He was one of those people.

Another guy I hired also came from a broken home. He had a distinctive smile because he was missing his front upper tooth. Our bank called one day asking to verify who this person was trying to cash a check, I told the teller to ask the customer to smile. The teller was confused. I repeated, "Ask him to smile." The teller did, saw the missing tooth, cracked up laughing and cashed my employee's check. After he proved himself, I sent him to a dentist to replace the missing tooth. What a huge difference this made in his attitude and ego.

I have taken chances on many people and I have few regrets. I think if a person has a good attitude with the ability and desire to learn, sometimes they just need a chance. If you can give it to them, it may be just the break they need.

TAKE ACTION:

- Tune in to your employees' needs. The "little things" you do to help can win their loyalty.

- Trust your gut when hiring. Give people a chance.

CHAPTER 14

Coaching & Mentoring

In previous chapters in this section, we talked about how it takes great people to build a great company. One way to help your people become great is to start a coaching and mentoring program.

Every new person in your company should have a mentor, regardless of their position. The day a new person comes on board, there should be someone they can go to with whom they feel comfortable so they can ask questions, discuss problems or just ask where to find something.

Once new employees feel more established in their positions, they will move up the career ladder in your organization. Then, they will need managerial coaches and mentors. Some companies engage the service of professional coaches. A career or business coach performs the same functions as a coach on a sports team. The coach encourages, counsels, cheers, offers suggestions, and provides guidance. If you set up relationships like these for your people, you will build a strong, close-knit team.

TAKE ACTION:

- Assign a mentor to every new employee in your company.

- Consider using professional coaches for your management team.

PART 4

Your Operations

Chapter 1 Safety Beyond Slogans 125

Chapter 2 Put Schedules "On the Wall" 131

Chapter 3 Smart Dispatching 133

Chapter 4 Job Sequencing 137

Chapter 5 Six Keys to Greater Productivity 139

Chapter 6 Production Incentives 143

Chapter 7 Equipment Standardization Saves Money 145

Chapter 8 Equipment Maintenance 149

Chapter 9 Stop Equipment Abuse with "Carrots" 151

Chapter 10 New Job Start-up Meetings 155

Chapter 11 Developing Bench Strength 159

Chapter 12 Quality is Not an Accident! 161

CHAPTER 1

Safety Beyond Slogans

Too often, companies talk about safety but that's as far as it goes – just talk. They hang safety slogans on the walls in their offices, but they don't stress safety in daily operations. Companies need more than slogans. Every landscape business needs a safety program and people committed to follow through with it. By taking action, you will show employees that you are serious about safety.

One way to begin is by contacting The Professional Landcare Network, known as PLANET. This national association of landscape contractors has a number of well thought-out safety programs, from their newest, called STARS, to the popular "100 tailgate meetings." My friend David Snodgrass, the chair of PLANET's industry development arm of the safety committee and the other members have done an incredible job in helping PLANET members in increasing safety awareness. PLANET provides members a comprehensive safety notebook and monthly safety newsletter called "Safety Scapes." (The safety information alone is worth the cost of membership.) If you are al-

ready a member, I hope you are using all of the resources PLANET offers.

Another economical and entertaining way to help your people learn about equipment safety is to show them any one of the many safety videos most manufacturers provide. PLANET has these videos in abundance, so check their Web site and catalog.

Trade journals like *Lawn & Landscape* connect landscape contractors with educational resources and provide safety articles you can share wtih employees. Once you have these resources (or videos), all you need is a TV with DVD/VCR capabilities. Make viewing these videos part of your annual safety program.

Some larger companies I work with have hired "safety companies," which are essentially hired watchdogs that ensure businesses are safe in every aspect. For example, one construction company I work with hired a safety company and gave them absolute authority to stop a job if they observed dangerous practices. This owner takes safety seriously.

If you want people in your company to be more safety conscious, post the number of days passed without a day missed because of an accident where everyone can see it. Update the sign every week. Some companies have incentive plans based on the number of days worked without an accident. Don't underestimate the power of an incentive plan. I have seen companies with a history of literally weeks of missed days in one year decrease accidents to only one or two days missed as a result of a simple incentive plan.

To make any plan a success, your company must hold weekly safety meetings. These meetings should last about 15 minutes each. Most companies like to have their meetings first thing Monday morning. That way, safety is on everyone's mind right at the beginning of the week. In a small company, everyone can meet in one group. In a larger company, organize meetings by crew or department. The key is to instill the message that safety is important in the minds of the entire team.

ValleyCrest Landscaping, headquartered in Calabasis, Calif., holds teleconference calls with all branch managers every Friday morning. If a manager had an accident in their branch during the prior week, he or she must describe what happened and how it will be prevented in the future.

How would you like to be a branch manager reporting a serious accident? Talk about peer pressure. ValleyCrest also assigns a new safety topic each week on a rotating basis to managers so each has an opportunity to participate. How can you start a proactive program like this?

There is one clear economic reason that companies should maintain spotless "safety records." The fewer accidents you have, the cheaper your insurance. It's as simple as that.

Now you may be wondering how insurance companies calculate your premiums. Every company has what is referred to as an MOD rate, short for modification rate. The MOD rate is issued by the National Council on Compensation Insurance Inc. (NCCI), headquartered in Boca Raton, Fla. The MOD rate is based on the amount and dollar value of workers' compensation claims filed against your company. So, NCCI is the neutral party that issues your rate.

The way it works is relatively simple. The first year in business, you start with a MOD rate of 1.00, or you pay 100 percent of the annual premium your insurance company charges. If there are accidents and losses, the MOD rate will increase to more than 100 percent, for example 1.1, which represents a 10 percent higher rate. If there are no accidents, the MOD rate will decrease. These percentages move up and down based on a preset formula the NCCI uses.

MOD rates are determined by on your company's three-year average experience. This will adjust each year based on your past experience. One company I work with had a series of accidents that caused their MOD to climb to 1.3 – that's a 30 percent higher premium per year! On the flip side, I work with another client that takes safety seriously. This company's MOD is less than 0.07, which is a 30-percent premium discount. The workers' compensation laws vary in each state, so check with your insurance agent for details.

To sum up, if you want to take accident prevention seriously, create an ongoing training program. The result will be fewer accidents and lower insurance premiums. Lastly, remember that having a good safety record doesn't happen by accident. It's up to you and your employees.

TAKE ACTION:

- Don't just talk about safety. Create a comprehensive safety program that covers every part of your business.

- Hold weekly safety meetings.

- If an accident occurs, discuss why it happened and how you can prevent future accidents.

- Contact PLANET to learn more about their safety information and programs.

CHAPTER 2

Put Schedules "On the Wall"

Scheduling and dispatching falls under planning, and many landscape owners don't like to plan. Because most small business owners work in the field, they do scheduling at the last minute. All of the information comes from what's in their head. As the company grows, this practice continues but can easily lead to a number of problems.

Companies that rely on last-minute planning and scheduling will end up with a "morning circus." Employees come to work in the morning not knowing which projects they are responsible for maintaining. Since they don't know what job they are going on, they don't know what equipment or materials they will need. I have seen up to 30 men scurry around the shop in the morning for more than one hour just trying to get organized so they can start the day. Talk about eating up the profits.

Here are some proven ways to alleviate this problem. First, write out a schedule and post it on a wall in a common area where it is visible to all employees. You can purchase a large schedule board or build one. If you want to save money and make it yourself, here is how. Purchase a 4-by-8 foot white board (the kind used for shower enclosures with a smooth, shiny surface on one side). Attach it to a wall horizontally where all of your team members can see it. Using thin black electrical tape (1/4 inch or so), divide the board into squares. (Draw a mock-up on paper first.) Across the top, list all of your crews; along the side write the days of the week. (You can flip-flop this arrangement if you choose.) Then, run a thin Velcro strip along the right side of the squares.

Next, buy small plastic cards about the size of credit cards or smaller. Color code the writing on the cards by category (i.e. employees might have black letters, trucks green and so on). On the back of each card, stick a small strip of Velcro so you can easily stick on and remove cards from the board. You can now place every person, vehicle and piece of equipment for the day on the squares and plan an entire week in advance. You can write in these squares with an erasable marker.

For example, week one will be on the left half, week two on the right.

At the end of week one, week three will take its place. This way, you will always have a complete schedule at least one week in advance.

Another practical idea is to keep an envelope for each crew member on the schedule board. Treat these as "mailboxes" for employees, and place messages or work orders in envelopes. That way, when employees come to work in the morning, they can check their envelope and note any important message for the day.

With the schedules up on the wall, crews will know which jobs they will be going on well in advance. This type of planning will help ease the "morning circus" and its associated frustrations, as well as reduce wasted time. In the long run, your company will be more efficient and, in turn, more profitable.

TAKE ACTION:

- Post crew schedules on the wall at least one week in advance.

- Plan equipment, labor and materials that each job will require in advance, and note this on your schedule board.

- Load equipment and materials the night before if possible.

- Make it a personal mission to stop the morning circus.

CHAPTER 3

Smart Dispatching

To dispatch your people more quickly each morning, crews should prepare the night before the equipment and materials they will need for the following day. When my crews came in at night, they tagged equipment that needed repairs and the mechanics would make sure it was ready to go by morning. As a result, much less spare equipment was needed, and the equipment lasted much longer because it was maintained regularly.

I had a part-time man work with my mechanics to ensure that all equipment was repaired and ready for the job site by morning. He was a full-time school custodian during the day and came in at 3 p.m. each afternoon. This arrangement worked perfectly for years. We had one day mechanic and two night mechanics. They performed maintenance on all equipment and fueled up trucks so everything was ready to go in the morning.

In the morning, my crew supervisors worked like jet airline pilots. They checked the schedule board, got the keys to their trucks, checked in with their managers, checked the oil in their vehicle and off they flew. It was like clockwork.

Owners have a million reasons why this "can't work," but it will. It doesn't happen by accident. You have to make it happen. Don't let the morning dispatch be more of a job than the work your employees will perform during the day. Confusion in the morning wastes time, demonstrates that the company is not organized, and tests everyone's patience.

Plenty of companies waste time in the morning preparing their trucks for the day. Materials are taken off the truck, put on the truck; tools are unloaded and loaded. Broken equipment comes off the trucks, and replacement equipment is put back on trucks Meanwhile, crew supervisors try to find out where they are working, look for directions to jobs and scribble down the information on scrap paper before shouting out orders. In one company I visited, I calculated that all this wasted time was costing the owner more than $110,000 per year. If any of this sounds familiar then it's time to change. Yes, it will require an investment to establish an organizational system, but every dollar invested will save several more dollars in terms of productivity and morale.

The best way to start is to delegate authority to one person and name them the dispatcher. If you have a small company, this "hat" probably falls on you.

The key is to get as much as possible done the night before. If you have a schedule board in the office, make sure you fill it out the night before so crews know where they are going the next day. Also, aim to complete routine maintenance, repairs, fueling and loading the night before. Think about what it costs when your people get fuel in the morning instead of at night. While crews wait in gas station lines in the morning, those minutes turn into hours and the hours turn into overtime. Think about how much wasted time like this adds up over the course of a year.

For example, if you have an average cost per crew member of $12.50 per hour (and I'll even include the labor burden in the $12.50), then add $6.25 for overtime, which totals $18.75 per hour. If there are four people in the truck, multiply that by four and the cost is $187.50 every morning just to get gas! This translates into thousands of dollars a year, and we haven't even talked about the crew stopping for coffee and donuts. The waste and lost revenue is stagger-

ing. If this scenario sounds familiar, put a stop to it immediately!

If you want to have a smooth-running operation, make one person responsible for the dispatching, plan the schedule in advance and post it up on the board. Then do repairs, maintenance and equipment changes the night before and prepare written directions and instructions for all jobs. If this is not happening now, figure out what you need to do to create a system similar to this.

Last but not least, let's not forget the keys. Make sure every driver gets in the habit of turning in keys and paperwork each night. Dedicate a separate key board next to the schedule board. This will help you quickly identify which trucks are still out at the end of the day. Identify each truck with a tag, then you'll know which crews are still out. Finally, get a cabinet that locks where you can keep at least two extra keys to every piece of equipment you own. This will prevent a problem when a driver loses, misplaces or goes home with the keys and doesn't report to work in the morning.

Every company and situation is different. You'll find a system that works for you. The most important thing is to create some method to the morning madness by organizing how you schedule and prepare for the following day.

TAKE ACTION:

- Fuel vehicles and gas cans at night, not in the morning.

- Manage all equipment maintenance and repairs in the evening so crews are ready to get out to worksites the next day.

- Load all materials and equipment the night before, if possible. Or, take care of this task in the early morning before crews arrive.

- Create written directions to job sites and prepare instructions before crews arrive to work in the morning.

- Keep duplicate keys in a locked place and require all drivers to place keys and paperwork in an assigned spot each night.

CHAPTER 4

Job Sequencing

After I had been in business for a few years with five crews working for me, I couldn't visit every job every day. This was frustrating to me because I knew that efficiency and quality were essential to making money and keeping customers happy. I knew that sometimes, when I wasn't there to oversee crews, jobs were not completed to my expectations.

One day in those early years, I pulled up to a large condominium complex and watched as the crews arrived. They parked their trucks and began unloading equipment in the worst possible place. This complex had 400 units and a large clubhouse, swimming pool and tennis courts. The crews chose to unload equipment in a small parking lot by the main entrance to the clubhouse. In a few hours, this area would be a busy place. It was also where the on-site manager's office was located. Yikes! I saw trouble.

As you might expect, as the crews unloaded equipment from the truck, they put it anywhere and everywhere. I looked at the site in utter disbelief. These were experienced guys. What

were they thinking?

As I watched, I got angry. But then I thought to myself, "Don't blame the guys because they were never taught what is expected. Blame yourself." I assumed they knew better, but they were not trained to be sensitive to what pleases customers and what doesn't. That day, I realized the need for job sequencing.

Job sequencing is performing a job in the right sequence so jobs are completed efficiently and effectively. I got to work outlining every detail, every action a maintenance or design/build supervisor would have to consider to do a job right. I knew I needed to communicate these responsibilities to every crewmember. In these days of "lean management," there aren't enough supervisors to watch every move in the field. So after making this job sequencing outline, I gathered the crews and explained my expectations. They got to work to make it happen.

The following are some of the issues we addressed:

- The best and most efficient place to park the truck.

- What equipment will be taken off the truck.
- Where gas cans should be placed to allow for efficient fueling.
- Who will operate each piece of equipment.
- When an equipment operator has completed the job, what he or she will do next.
- What the proper sequence of the work will be. (For example: whether grass trimming and edging be completed before the mowing or after.)
- When and where lunch and work breaks will be taken.

This all sounds like basic stuff, but how many landscapers work each day without any kind of process or order? Lack of process can easily lead to inconsistency, which leads to confusion, which leads to a lack of productivity, which leads to low profit margins, which leads to decreased quality, which leads to unhappy customers. You get the picture.

If you don't have a system, you need to create one. It's best if every crew performs their work basically the same way. They should think about sequence: what order to perform each task for optimum efficiency.

Gather your people and ask them to detail the best way to complete each job. Then, as jobs progress during the season, meet on a regular basis and discuss necessary improvements. Ask a manager to observe jobs in progress and offer an opinion on the job sequencing. Get everyone on the same page and thinking about efficiency.

TAKE ACTION:

- Create questions for your crews to think about in order to promote the best job sequencing and efficiency.

- Have crews detail in writing the best way to complete each job.

- Observe each job and review the job sequencing. What worked and what didn't? Constantly aim for improvement.

CHAPTER 5

Six Keys to Greater Productivity

When I hear the word "production" I think of how the work is being done and how much of it is getting done. There are many books on the general subject of production, but only a few of them apply to production in the landscape industry.

A report recently published by the Crystal Ball Committee of PLANET offers excellent advice on the subject. The report reviews many ways to improve production in your company. I am not going to attempt to duplicate their efforts. Instead, I boiled it down to six keys for improving production in your operation.

1. Hire right.
All your work is done by people, so hire the best you can possibly afford. When I say hire right, I mean hire quick learners, smart people with common sense and positive attitudes. Are these qualities difficult to find in people? Yes, but not impossible. Great companies are made up of great people, and they don't get there by accident. Great people work with great companies because these companies searched for them. Go find your great people.

2. Purchase quality equipment.
Your people need reliable equipment to do their work. It is very frustrating to work with equipment that breaks down. Labor costs more than equipment. So purchase the best you can afford, and y ou will reduce the amount of labor required to get the job done. Eventually, this translates into higher gross margins.

3. Educate your people.
It is so important to educate your people. Quality equipment and great people make no difference if you don't invest in training them to use equipment properly. This education takes time and costs money, but the investment is essential to reach maximum productivity. Set up a training program. Also, be sure to train your people the right way. Follow the "OTC" process: Orient them on equipment and the job; Train them on what and how to do; and then Certify that they know their jobs by testing and observing.

4. Clarify expectations and communicate well.

Communicate with your people all the time. In my consulting work, I meet crews all over the country that work week after week with no one talking to them about their performance. No one asks them if there is a way to help them work smarter. No one asks whether equipment is up to snuff. No one discusses efficiency and the attitudes of their fellow crewmembers. If you want top production, meet with your people and ask them how to get it. It's not a secret. They know. And if you ask, they will want to offer their suggestions.

5. Track the productivity of your jobs.

Remember, what gets tracked or measured gets done. If your people don't know what the production goal is, how can they meet it? And if you don't track performance and progress, how will you know what's getting done, how well and in what time frame?

6. Reward peak performers.

If there is no incentive for improved performance, then why would your people want to try to out-perform your budget? They will come to work each day, but that's it. Give workers real incentives – not the once-a-year holiday bonus that is forgotten as soon as the check is cashed. Offer employees incentives for beating production goals. Give them a reason to track their own production and reward them with something meaningful. Cash is always an appealing reward. If they help you make more money, then share some of that with them. But rewards for good performance don't always have to be in the form of money. A sincere "thanks" once in a while for a job well done goes a long way. And it doesn't hurt to give workers praise in front of others.

TAKE ACTION:

Follow these six principles to improve your production and profits.

- Hire the right people.

- Purchase quality equipment.

- Educate your people.

- Clarify your expectations and communicate with your employees.

- Create a job cost system.

- Reward peak performers.

CHAPTER 6

Production Incentives

The goal of an incentive program is to motivate workers and help them think more like business owners. When I was in business, I instinctively wanted to find a way to increase productivity. Chances are, your people do not think the same way.

I wanted to make more profit and was willing to share it with people who worked harder. After 15 years in business, I took a stab at my first incentive program. What I set up was very simple. For every hour the crew could save on budgeted hours, I paid them a predetermined amount of money they could divide among themselves. My production immediately increased as a result. In fact, in the first month we improved our company's productivity by up to 20 percent some days. It made me wonder what the crews were doing before I initiated the program.

Before you can start an incentive system, you must determine an accurate way to track production. If there are too many jobs to track individually, the jobs can be tracked together as long as you have the total hours needed to perform all jobs. The key is to give your crew supervisors the budgeted hours for each job; believe me, they will find innovative ways to save hours.

Quality was a big issue for us. If a crew saved hours and didn't produce quality, the customers would be upset. We would end up doing the job again, which does nothing to improve production. One way to encourage efficiency and quality is to send the crew back. Track the time they spend fixing the job, and double that time. Those extra hours serve as penalty in this particular incentive system.

The key is consistency. Don't start and stop an incentive program. You also can't change the bonus formula if employees begin to win. Stick to your word, and reward employees with the incentive you promise. Remember, you're the one who made the rules. And these labor savings ultimately save your company money, improve efficiency and increase profitability.

Systems will drive employees' behavior, so be sure your incentive programs encourages the behavior you want. If your system is fair, everyone will win.

TAKE ACTION:

- Consider an incentive system based on labor hours saved.

- Make sure job estimates are specific and hours can be accurately tracked.

- Pay your employees the incentives you promise them.

CHAPTER 7

Equipment Standardization Saves Money

I recently worked with a landscape contractor whose company does design/build and grounds maintenance. Most of his $1.5 million sales per year came from the residential segment of the market. Before we hit the books, he wanted me to see his shop, where he housed trucks and equipment. I could tell he was proud of his equipment. He had every right to be because he cared for it meticulously. The trucks were clean and shiny. I asked him how many full-time maintenance crews he employed, and he said three.

As I looked closer at the mowers, I noticed he used several different brands. The same was true of his backpack blowers and string trimmers. I asked why he had so many different brands, he said they were all great deals.

Deals are good, but not when you must buy so many different brands. A review of his profit and loss statement showed he was paying various equipment repair dealers a small fortune to keep his equipment running. Because he had so many different kinds of equipment, he figured it made no sense to stock parts. Funny thing is, he did this for years, just accepting the high cost of parts and repairs. He could never get equipment serviced by just one dealer.

This is an extreme example, but what would an inspection of your shop reveal? The lesson: Do your homework before purchasing equipment. If you take a tour of some of the large landscape companies. you will find that most use as few brands as possible. Why? Many reasons.

First, your dealer will be more loyal to you because of larger-volume purchases. Second, it is easier to stock parts when you are buying the same brand. (Also, you can strip old equipment for parts.) Finally, mechanics become familiar with common repairs and preventive maintenance. Your crews can use the same equipment interchangeably. And it's just safer to stick to a couple of brands. Crews that use the same equipment every day become more proficient in operating the equipment, so fewer accidents occur.

Now, let's take a quick look at equipment for an entirely different industry: airlines. Southwest Airlines is the most profitable carrier in the United States today, and one of the main reasons is equipment standardization. As of November 2006, Southwest flew 479 jets and all were Boeing 737s. This strategy makes sense for their business, and it makes sense for the landscape industry, too.

Can one manufacturer provide the best of every type of equipment? Probably not. But you should try to standardize whenever possible because there are many advantages. At least try to stick to one mower brand, whether the models are walk-behinds, riding mowers or zero-turn mowers. Then, choose one brand of two-cycle equipment.

When I was in business, we only purchased one brand of mower. Because of this, I could team up with landscape contractors in other states and make group purchases. In one case, I remember saving close to 25 percent on each mower.

Even for design/build contractors who require larger equipment, it makes sense to stay with one brand of backhoe or front-end loader. And don't even get me started on trucks. There are so many brands available, and many are excellent. But the same principle applies.

Do your homework. Look beyond the purchase price and consider ease of maintenance and potential repair costs. You don't want to purchase equipment that will spend its life in the shop.

The other mistake contractors make is purchasing too much equipment. Contractors just love machines. I have a client that does a considerable amount of excavation. On a recent visit, I walked his "yard" with him and noticed he had a lot of equipment – most of it just sitting. I asked him what his equipment utilization rate was. He looked at me like I had two heads and replied, "Utilization rate? I have no idea. I just love this stuff. I love to buy it, fix it, paint it and keep it."

After a closer look, it turned out some pieces were only used a few weeks each year; some pieces were not used at all. He had invested tens of thousands of dollars in equipment that just sat. Some of it was literally rusting away.

Is this happening to you? If you think it is, I recommend that you conduct an audit to figure out your utilization rate. If you are a small contractor, you're going to tell me you use everything every single day, and that's great. But for larger contractors, I doubt this is the case.

Here's a tip: The next time you need to purchase a utility truck, buy one that is one size bigger and heavier-duty than you think you need. We all have a tendency to think that the truck we select is big enough or sturdy enough until we begin to use it every day. Federal and state weight laws are getting more and more restrictive. And, one thing is for sure. You can deal with a truck that is one size too big, but it's murder getting the job done with one that's too small.

TAKE ACTION:

- Choose a few equipment brands you trust and be loyal to those brands.

- Stock parts and manage routine maintenance and repair in-house, if possible.

- Don't purchase trucks or equipment unless you will use them. Figure out your utilization rate and refer to it before you buy.

CHAPTER 8

Equipment Maintenance

Owners and managers usually do not do enough to make sure their team members appreciate equipment. Conscientious operators will extend the life of their equipment considerably. As an owner, your job is to build awareness of just how valuable equipment is. Tell crewmembers how much your equipment costs. They also need to know what their role is in maintaining the equipment. Let them know they must check oil and replace belts frequently, and also report any changes in performance. Damage should be pointed out to supervisors immediately. Even if operators don't maintain equipment themselves, they should understand how it is done.

It's been my observation that owners and managers are fairly conscientious about maintaining their equipment. But when some companies are busy, they get into the bad habit of waiting for a rainy day to take care of service needs. Equipment maintenance should be managed at the end of the workday and on a regularly scheduled basis, as specified by the manufacturer.

Also, if your crews are working 40-plus hour weeks and performing maintenance at overtime rates, you are paying a hefty price. Keep in mind, if your team members do maintenance work at the end of the day when they are tired, you risk lower quality work – tired people want to go home, not turn wrenches. So hire a qualified part-time technician to perform routine maintenance. A trained technician will do a better, more efficient job (and generally have their own tools, which is another savings). And, if you stock common parts, the technician will be able to fix most problems right on the spot.

Some owners say they want to hire a technician, but they can't find one who is qualified. Most professional technicians start their day early in the morning and finish no later than 4 p.m. But every technician I've known does work on the side for friends, neighbors and other businesses to earn extra money. Find one of these professionals at a new or used car dealership or construction equipment company. Many of these technicians would love to have a steady part-time job with flexible hours and the chance to supplement their income.

At first blush, you might think hiring a professional is too expensive because he or she will charge more per hour than you pay crewmembers. But what is the cost of not having a good technician on board? If you send the equipment to the dealership, repairs will cost you three times what you would pay a mechanic, plus the mark-up on parts.

Once you find the right person for the job, you will wonder how you ever got along without a technician.

TAKE ACTION:

• Manage equipment maintenance on a regular basis.

• Find a part-time professional mechanic to do the maintenance work.

• Stock common parts so repairs can be done each night.

CHAPTER 9

Stop Equipment Abuse with "Carrots"

Almost all landscape companies have problems with loss or abuse of equipment and tools. Most of the time, the damage or loss is not intentional. Workers leave shovels, tape measures, brooms and even expensive equipment on a jobsite. In a recent renovation of my own home, I had to tell electricians that they left expensive testing equipment behind. Painters left ladders; carpenters left tools. I even had window washers leave their squeegees. What in the world am I going to do with them? Clean my own windows? With the cost of equipment as high as it is today, you would think these professionals would be more careful.

Sometimes, angry workers will take out their frustration on equipment and tools. Others just plain disregard proper use. I have seen equipment being taken off trucks without using the ramps – bouncing two and three feet in the air before they hit the ground! I have witnessed large mowers being run off curbs without ramps. I have seen equipment operators deliberately run over rocks so they could break the machine and go home early or get a different job. I

don't know about you, but this raises my blood pressure 50 points!

Leaving equipment unattended on jobs is another problem. You won't believe this one. I was standing on the sidewalk by my office in the inner city talking to an equipment salesman when two guys pulled up in an old blue van. The guys approached us, saying they had a brand new 8-horsepower leaf blower for sale for $50. When I said I wasn't interested, the one guy repeated again, "Only 50 bucks, do you want to see it?" I said no again, much more emphatically so he got the point, returned to his van and drove away. The salesman and I just shook our heads.

A half hour later I went back inside my office only to receive a phone call from my crew supervisor on the other side of the city. He said our new 8-horsepower leaf blower was missing. You guessed it. That was my blower in the back of the van! Unfortunately, the two scam artists got away with it.

What is even worse is when there is a thief within your company. When I first started my business, an employee hid a string trimmer and backpack blower in some high grass at the edge of the parking lot of a small shopping center we maintained. This was the last job of the day. When he came back to the shop, he told us the equipment was stolen. We all went back for a second look. I returned to the stores on the property and asked if anyone had seen anythinig suspicious.

To my surprise, a receptionist at one of the stores told me she saw "my guy" put the equipment in the high grass. She pointed to where he hid the equipment. But then she added, "I don't think you're going to find it. Another group of guys saw your guy hide it, and after he left, they took the equipment."

Can anything be done about this? Yes. Hire people with good attitudes and values. Employees with bad attitudes almost always cause problems. Of course, this is easy to say, but when you are so busy you don't know which way is up, it's difficult to take time to screen employees for bad attitudes. When interviewing potential employees, try to detect what type of person you are dealing with. My motto is, "Hire for attitude and teach the skills." Skills can be taught but it's very difficult to change a person's attitude.

Other suggestions: Hold one person on each crew accountable for all tools and equipment. Unless responsibility is assigned, very few employees will care if equipment is left on the job or abused. Find a secure place to store the equipment at night and while on the job. In many new companies, tools and equipment are kept in a common unlocked area. Crews deposit their equipment and tools at the end of the day in this area and re-load what they need in the morning. There is virtually no way to secure the equipment this way. Big mistake.

The best method I have found is a combination of personal responsibility, a secure place to store equipment and the "proverbial carrot." (That's the incentive.)

First, create bins so each crew can lock equipment in a secure area. Next, make a list of all equipment along with the cost of each item. Keep one copy of the list in your office and the other on one of the walls in the secured area. You keep one key and give another to the crewmember in charge. Finally, give an incentive (the carrot) to the "key holder." For example, offer $500 per year for taking the responsibility. The incentive must be large enough to be meaningful, but it also has to make financial sense for the company.

Now it's simple, at the end of the season or at a predetermined time, check the equipment and tools against your list. If there is anything missing, subtract the cost from the incentive money. The key-holder gets the balance.

Some companies use secure trailers to store the equipment. This solves the problem of keeping equipment secure and saves loading and unloading time each morning and evening. This might be something for you to consider.

When our company used the bonus program I just described, we also included damages to the vehicle and equipment. If you include these, make sure to adjust the (carrot) incentive. One caution, if your crews switch equipment too often, this system may not work for you. I advise against mixing crews and equipment because it is too difficult to hold your crew supervisors accountable for loss and damage. It's best to assign the same equipment and vehicles to the same people every day.

This incentive method dramatically reduced my loss of equipment and tools, as well as abuse and vehicle damage.

Are you angry that you are thinking of having to institute such a program? Upset that you can't just trust your people? If you are, you have a right to be. Most owners feel it's the crew supervisor's responsibility to care for equipment; they are getting paid more for it. But human nature is human nature. I gave up the fight, created this program and it worked.

Will it cost you money? Yes. Will it save you money? I think so. From my experience your productivity should improve. Think about it. You have all your equipment and tools on the job all the time. Because of this incentive program, we virtually eliminated tool loss and abuse and had better looking vehicles. And as a bonus, our theft problem disappeared. Our crewmembers were happier, our crew supervisors were satisfied and I was relieved to not have to worry about this problem.

TAKE ACTION:

- List equipment and tools for each crew along with the cost of each piece.

- Assign one person to be responsible for equipment.

- Create an incentive as a reward for securing equipment and keeping it in clean and good working order.

CHAPTER 10

New Job Start-up Meetings

Whether you do landscape maintenance or design/build work, it's a good idea to have a new job startup meeting before you start a new project. This is especially important for construction or large maintenance jobs. Once the job is awarded to you, make it clear to your customers that you want them to attend this meeting. At the meeting, you have the opportunity to introduce your key people, brief customers and your crew members on what to expect, and resolve any questions.

As the owner, it is best if you attend the meeting with your people, but as you grow and have too many jobs for that to be practical, assign the account manager, operations manager or crew supervisor to this task.

A new job start-up meeting sends a strong message to customers that you mean business and are serious about quality, clarity and customer satisfaction. It also sets a precedent for future meetings.

There are other important reasons to have this meeting and other regular job meetings as the project progresses. Mainly, the open communication will resolve customer concerns. But also, as the job progresses, these meetings will allow you to ensure your customers' expectations are being met. In addition, an intial meeting firmly establishes who the contact person is in case customers need to ask questions.

People like to deal with a single contact when possible. Let me give you an example of one hotel that understands this. While on vacation with my family in Old Quebec City, Canada, we stayed at the renowned Fairmont Le Chateau Frontenac. After we checked in and went to our rooms, we had some questions about where to eat in the hotel. I went to the telephone, but noticed that unlike other hotels, there was only one help button marked, "guest services." I thought that was unusual.

I pressed the button and was promptly greeted by a friendly and charming lady. She told me that she was there to help in any way she could. I asked her questions about the restaurants in the hotel. She offered information about restaurants in the hotel as well as other eateries in the city. She even volunteered to make reservations for us. She ended the conversation by informing me that she would be our daytime contact while we were guests of the hotel and to call anytime.

After a few days, my wife and I wanted to enjoy a leisurely dinner. So we called her to arrange for a hotel babysitter. She cheerfully complied and made our restaurant reservations. We were impressed. Before we left the hotel we felt compelled to meet her and say thanks. We will never forget that vacation, or her. From that experience I learned how powerful a single contact person can be.

Make it clear to your clients who the contact person is that will handle their job. Make sure your contact person understands his responsibilities to the customer.

Now back to the new job startup meeting. Before you conclude, establish a date for your next job meeting. These subsequent meetings will provide a friendly, informal forum to talk about the project and resolve problems. At this time, you can also present customers with invoices, review change orders and, most importantly, accept checks for invoices due.

Another important method to ensure customer satisfaction is to have your customer agree that if there are any problems, they will promise to let you know immediately. You want to establish a "don't complain to others, tell us" policy. Your customer needs to know that you want them to be totally happy with the job, and the only way you can assure this is by regular communication.

I frequently stay in Sheraton Hotels because I love their service promise: "If you're not satisfied, we're not satisfied." What a great slogan. Sheraton's service promise ensures that you will have a great stay. They tell you at check-in if there is anything they can do, just tell us or dial "O." At checkout, they ask, "Did you have a perfect stay?" If not, they will make amends. I have experienced that first-hand.

Back to your jobsite meetings. For large commercial and corporate jobs it is advisable to have three tiers of management attend. Involve all crew supervisors, managers and anyone responsible for carrying out the job. This way, in case the person you report to or their boss leaves or gets promoted, you will not be a stranger to the others. One sure way contractors lose jobs is when the customer contact person, or "Mr. Big," is promoted or disappears.

When dealing with commercial projects, you may find that many new managers like to bring in vendors they already know and trust. If your company worked with old management, be sure to get an agreement at the new job startup meeting that if any of the managers change positions, it will automatically trigger a meeting so you can meet the "new player." You will find that they will understand exactly what you are talking about and generally agree without much trouble.

One caution: Don't waste time briefing the big boss on details of the job unless he or she wants to hear the nitty-gritty. Use the meeting for introduction purposes, to learn all you can about them and what they expect. Then tell "Mr. Big" how much you appreciate the time he or she took out of the busy day and that you can now discuss job details with "your contact person." If they are really busy, they will remember and love you for this.

One last thought: Before you start the job, get permission to take "before" and "after" pictures. People have short memories and when renewal time comes, it's great to have pictures to remind them what the property previously looked like. Having some before photos saved many contracts for my business. It's also great to get permission to use these pictures for your marketing initiatives.

If you hold new job start-up and regular update meetings as each job progresses, you will ensure happy customers who will spread the word to their friends and associates. It doesn't get better than that!

TAKE ACTION:

- Assign only one contact person for each client.

- Set up a "new job start-up meeting" to meet key players who will be involved in the project.

- Have an automatic meeting if there are any changes of your contact or "Mr. Big."

- Ensure that both parties understand all expectations.

- Agree that any problems or requests immediately come to your attention for resolution.

CHAPTER 11

Developing Bench Strength

Bench strength is a sports term that refers to having players "on the bench" waiting and ready to get in the game. These are coaches' back-up players. Baseball teams can't win games with just one or two great pitchers, and we can't depend on just one or two key people to run our companies.

Small owner-operator companies depend on crew supervisors to do the work. If they are to grow and move to the next level, the owner needs a right-hand person to help. Oftentimes, this person comes from the ranks of the crew supervisors.

As growth occurs, the owner must continue to develop people who can manage the work and manage others. It is a painful process in the early years of a company. Because the company is strained from growth, the pool of people to choose from is limited. If a crew supervisor doesn't come to work, the only one on the bench is the owner. That's no way to run a company, but it's a reality.

It may sound idealistic to offer advice about developing bench strength when a company is in this position. But the best thing an owner can do is bring in qualified people to help ease the situation and allow for growth. Many companies are stalled at this level. The owners say they can't find anyone, but the reality is in many cases, they don't want to spend the money to attract higher-caliber workers. As you know, it's not easy to find and hire good people, but they are out there.

If a company is ever to have bench strength, the owner must line up someone on the bench as a replacement and continue to build the company in this manner. Then they can begin to cross-train and hire people as "backups." This is one of the toughest but most important parts of operating a successful landscape company. Experience has taught me that the owner has to think about and work on this every day.

Let me give you two ways to help develop bench strength. The first is to always hire people who are qualified to do more than what you need. Even when hiring production people for your maintenance crews, try to hire someone who could become an assistant supervisor or even a supervisor one day. Always consider whether the candidates you are interviewing can do more than the job they are applying for.

Second, don't be afraid to hire people smarter in areas where you are weak. As a matter of fact, hire the smartest, most talented people you can find and afford. Your company needs a variety of people with different knowledge, skills and experience.

As an owner or manager, know what your strengths and weaknesses are and hire people to cover those weakness. We've talked about this before. Diverse people create well-rounded teams, which allows you the opportunity to manage growth and deal with adversity. When I was in business, one of my biggest regrets was not hiring a president to replace me. I realize now, if I had done this I could have focused on my strengths and been far more effective.

Another equally important reason for developing bench strength is that it creates value in your company. If people are your company's most valuable asset, and you have great people who handle their jobs with competency, then not only do you have bench strength, you have created value. Buyers are willing to pay for this.

If and when you decide to sell your company, buyers will not only look at the financials, but also at your people. Buyers purchase accounts but are equally interested in your people. We all know that employees are as difficult to find and develop as customers. So treat your people with care. Work with them, educate them, encourage them, reward them and cross-train them so, ultimately, you have bench strength in your company.

TAKE ACTION:

• Hire people with potential to grow in your company.

• Seek out and hire the smartest, most talented people.

• Hire employees that are strong where you are weak.

• Cross-train your people and develop "bench strength."

CHAPTER 12

Quality is Not an Accident!

In 1979 Phillip B. Crosby wrote the book, *Quality Is Free*. His book helped us understand what the term quality means by saying it can be substituted with the phrase "conformance to requirements." He explains that to have quality or conformance to requirements, there must be a way to measure the quality one is trying to achieve. He adds, "Quality management is a systematic way of guaranteeing that organized activities happen the way they are planned."

The subject of quality is poorly understood. When customers say they want a "quality job," the quality they are talking about really depends on their expectations and requirements. Once this is understood, guaranteeing that the organized activities will happen to assure quality is the challenge.

In my experience, I have found that quality has a different meaning for a residential customer than for a corporate customer. A commercial customer refers to a "quality landscape contractor" when they deliver a 100 percent reliable and fast, "no excuse" service. Residential customers, on the other hand, are usually more lenient about service but expect absolute quality of workmanship and materials. Please understand that this is not a hard and fast rule, but it's generally true. The point is, it's extremely important to understand how each customer defines quality.

Once you understand your customers and their expections, the best way to maintain quality on a consistent basis is to establish a grading system so you can identify quality. If you are a maintenance contractor, create a list of every area in the landscape (i.e. lawn, shrubs, trees, shrub beds, etc.). Next to each item, put the numbers 1 through 5, or 1 through 10 if you like. The numbers will represent levels of quality; the higher the number, the better the quality. Now, figure out with your people what level of quality the numbers stand for. For example, if a 10 stands for a totally weed-free, thick green lawn, then what would an eight or five represent?

With this simple tool in hand, regularly (preferably monthly) inspect your customers' properties. When I say inspect, I don't mean a "drive by," but a complete inspection. Once this is done for a few months, the numbers will take on meaning and the level of quality of each property will be established.

If you are not a maintenance contractor, you will need to create a quality system that monitors the results of your work. A similar type of numeric system can be created; just adapt it to what makes sense for your operation. The principles are the same regardless of the type of work your company does.

Now this is not a foolproof method, but it does work. I know contractors who use it successfully. The reason it doesn't work for many companies is because it requires time and discipline. I began to use this system in my company, and I can testify that it works. But I also can tell you it requires commitment to see the payoff.

Once established, you will be able to determine which crews produce the best work. Contests with prizes or bonuses can be given for the highest scores. Crews with consistently low scores may have a problem with either lack of knowledge, experience or ambition. Whatever the problem, you can address it.

Once this system is perfected, you can use it as a tool in the sales process with your customers to determine the level of quality they expect.

For example, explain to your customer that it's not easy to have a weed-free lawn, especially if it is a large one. Of course, it is possible, but it's more expensive and usually unnecessary. It's your job to determine how many weeds in the lawn they will tolerate.

And what about the color of the turf? A deep-green lawn is not always important to commercial customers. Many are happy as long as there are no weeds in the shrub beds, the lawn looks reasonable and everything is neat and litter-free. Once you understand what customers want, you can educate crews to meet your customers' expectations.

Before I understood these simple principles, we lost some really great accounts. And worse, in some cases, we didn't make the money we could have because I wanted my people to perform at a higher-quality level than the customers wanted.

Let me tell you this story. One of my clients was a wealthy guy who purchased a very large residential property in Greenwich, Conn., as an investment. It was about 35 acres total with two houses and 10 acres of turf. The base contract for the grounds maintenance was more than $50,000 per year. We maintained the property for two years, and in each of those years he spent an additional $75,000 on improvements.

Why did I lose this customer? Although he lived on the grounds only a few weeks each year, he loved the herb garden that was next to the main house. On a walk of the property, he showed me the garden and pointed out the weeds and general disorder. I had not figured anything into the contract for work in this area, but I told my account manager to have the crews weed the garden while they were there. Did they weed the garden? Yes. Did they do a great job?

No. Did the garden look like what my client wanted? No. Bottom line, he visited the property a few weeks later, was disappointed, and we were given a 30-day termination notice.

Was he a temperamental customer? Yes. But it was my fault for not reading his expectations correctly. I goofed. In retrospect, I should have had my people make that little herb garden absolutely perfect. He would have paid the extra cost without question. I failed to see what was important in his eyes and lost a great account.

I believe in Phillip Crosby's book title, *Quality Is Free*. It really is cheaper to do a quality job right the first time. The General Electric Company proved this beyond a doubt when former CEO Jack Welch instituted his Six Sigma program. They invested millions into their quality program, but the cost was only a fraction of the additional profits they earned as a result.

Whether talking about a large manufacturing company or your small, family-owned landscape company, quality is everyone's concern. Educate all your people in the ways of attaining it. It doesn't cost any more to produce quality, but it can reap large rewards.

TAKE ACTION:

- From the very beginning, try to understand your customers' quality expectations.

- Create a system to monitor the quality of your accounts.

- Use your quality grading system to further understand the level of quality your customers expect and are willing to pay for.

- Let employees know that only quality services and materials are acceptable to your company.

PART 5

Acquiring Your Customers

Chapter	1	Sales, Advertising, Marketing, Help!	167
Chapter	2	I Don't Need a Marketing Plan, Do I?	169
Chapter	3	Your Marketing Calendar	173
Chapter	4	Networking Works	175
Chapter	5	Keep Referrals Rolling in the Door	177
Chapter	6	Are Your Business Cards in Your Pocket?	179
Chapter	7	First Sell to Your Customers	181
Chapter	8	Cold Calling, a Chilling Prospect?	183
Chapter	9	Trust Me – Great Proposals Build Trust	185
Chapter	10	Managing Your Sales Staff	189
Chapter	11	How Do You Pay Your Sales People?	193
Chapter	12	Put Your Logos on Everything	197
Chapter	13	Direct Mail Works	199
Chapter	14	Telemarketing	201
Chapter	15	Newspaper & Magazine Ads	203
Chapter	16	Yellow Pages Ads	205
Chapter	17	Advertising Materials	207
Chapter	18	Do You Need a Web Site?	209

CHAPTER 1

Sales, Advertising, Marketing, Help!

There is much confusion among the terms sales, advertising and marketing. So before we begin this section, let me clarify. Here are some simple definitions of these words and how they are used in the green industry.

- Marketing is a general term that includes programs to reach target prospects. The programs or plans could include advertising, public relations, direct mail, networking and more. We'll explore this further in following chapters.

- Sales or selling describes the activity where you have one-on-one meetings, make telephone calls, network and meet with prospects and customers to sell them a service or product.

- Advertising is a sales tactic or method to attract prospects who are unfamiliar or "cold" to your products or services. Advertising can be a part of a marketing program that might also include direct mail, public relations, your company Web site and more.

A successful marketing program is balanced to include sales tactics that attract people unfamiliar to your product or services, and sales tactics that follow-up and reinforce initial efforts. Finally, there are more direct efforts in which you try to generate a proposal and then close a sale.

Here is a practical and simplistic example: First, a direct mail piece goes to a potential customer's home. Second, a follow-up call to the prospect is made to stimulate and ascertain interest. Third, if there is interest, a visit is made. A proposal is delivered and hopefully, a contract is secured.

Now that these terms are clear, the following chapters will address a common goal all professional landscape company owners share – acquiring great customers.

TAKE ACTION:

- Marketing is a general term encompassing sales, advertising, direct mail, etc.

- Successful marketing programs have a balance of tactics to generate interest to lead to a sale.

CHAPTER 2

I Don't Need a Marketing Plan, Do I?

Some time ago I spoke at a green industry convention in the Boston area with 650 business owners in attendance. My topic was sales and marketing. At the beginning of my presentation, I asked the group for a show of hands of how many had created a marketing plan. After some coaxing, hands went up and I counted a total of 13 individuals.

My follow-up question to the 13 owners was, "Honestly now, how many of you have used the plan during the past 12 months to guide your company?" A total of five owners sheepishly raised their hands. I asked those five if they had reviewed the plan after 12 months to determine what worked and what didn't, so they could make appropriate changes for the next season. The answer was two. Two out of 650 business owners were effectively using their marketing plans to grow their business!

Truthfully, I was not surprised. This is typical of companies in the green industry. In fact, I was once one of those company owners. During the first 24 years I was in business, I didn't have a plan either. I ran the company by the seat of my pants.

It wasn't until the last six years when I hired a marketing director that I finally put a marketing plan down in writing. OK, so now you might be thinking, "I can't afford to hire someone because I am too small." You're probably right. Or, maybe you believe that you don't have time or don't know how to create a marketing plan, but these are not good excuses. Whether you have been in business for one year or 20 years, you need to have a marketing plan; even if it's a simple one.

When you have a well thought-out plan, your improve the chances of working for the right customers in the right markets, and selling the right products and services. You will also be able to figure out what types of work yield the highest profit margins.

Let me give you some examples. In my consulting practice, when I begin working with a new landscape business owner, one of the things I look at is their market area and what work will bring this company the highest margins. You might think that most companies would be persuing the highest profit margin work, but that is not true. I know of companies that believe they should work close to their home base. Because of this, they have limited success. What they don't realize is if they drove just 30 minutes more, they could charge 25 percent more per hour. Why don't they travel? They just never took the time to think about it.

Many companies offer basic spring and fall cleanups, mulching, weeding, pruning and mowing. Is there money in these areas? Yes, but nowhere near the amount of money that other more lucrative services can bring in. Why do some owners seem stuck doing these basic things instead of performing work that really makes money? Again, I think they just haven't thought it through; they have no plan.

Even when I had my own company, I didn't realize until I was in business for more than 20 years that there was just as much if not more profit in industrial work than in other arenas. Most landscape contractors, including myself, assumed that the industrial sites didn't spend any money because their grounds didn't look as nice as corporate or commercial properties. Boy, was I wrong.

Our large industrial accounts, although much more conservative in their approach, wanted just one supplier and were loyal to us as long as we delivered them good service. As a result, the profit margins were higher. During my last five years in business, our large industrial accounts delivered substantially higher gross margins than corporate clients, and with a lot fewer headaches. And the bonus

– I literally had no competition because my fellow landscape contractors didn't want this work.

The moral of the story is, take the time to study your market opportunities, challenge your assumptions, and plan your future.

Let me give you an actual example of what I mean and the "power of planning." One small landscape contractor I worked with never had a marketing plan. After acknowledging the importance of this type of planning, he agreed to spend a day with me during the winter to create one. We reviewed his company's strengths, weaknesses, opportunities, threats, current customers, potential market, competitors and so on. All the aspects of a plan including pricing.

At the end of the day, a much clearer picture and vision began to emerge for the direction of his company. Part of this vision was to have a more substantial maintenance business to serve as an anchor so he could protect the business from future economic downturns. To accomplish this, we agreed it would make sense to transition from his current customer base to more affluent communities less than 30 minutes away. As part of the plan, we wrote a simple advertising campaign to create awareness in these new markets. At the same time, we asked for referrals from current customers who lived near the target area.

Did the marketing plan work? Yes. By the end of the season, he had increased sales by more than 70 percent!

Interestingly, his number of clients didn't increase, but sales volume did. Here's why. When we wrote the plan, we decided to follow the 80/20 rule. We made a list of all his current customers and ranked them according to sales volume and profitability. My advice to him in light of our new plan was to either significantly raise prices for those in the bottom 20 percent, or drop them. (In either case, this must be done professionally.) He agreed to do this, but reluctantly.

Did he lose accounts? Yes, but time was freed up for his crews to focus on more profitable work. Additionally, these new accounts spent a considerable amount of money improving their properties, which increased his annual sales.

Now he was really making money. At the end of the season, he clearly saw the wisdom in the plan and became a true believer. The moral of the story is to take the needed time and plan your future.

TAKE ACTION:

- Take the time to create a marketing plan.

- Bring in outside professionals if needed.

- Use the plan; review it at least quarterly.

CHAPTER 3

Your Marketing Calendar

The first time I heard the term "marketing calendar" was in the early 1990s during a presentation on marketing presented by author and marketer extraordinare, Jay Levinson. If you don't recognize the name, you may recognize his books. He is the author of *Guerrilla Marketing* and numerous other "gorilla" books, including *Guerrilla Marketing Weapons* and *Guerrilla Marketing Attack.*

Levinson explained in his talk that he was on the team that made Marlboro cigarettes the most popular cigarette brand in the world. (He was proud of his accomplishment, but said that his success was bittersweet in light of later medical findings about smoking and cancer.)

Toward the end of his speech, Levinson explained how as part of a marketing plan, you must include a one-page marketing calendar. It is a simple concept. List every week in the year in a column on the left, and across the top write down items that you could use in your marketing plan for the year. Next to each item, leave a space for the cost of the initiative. On this one sheet, you will know when every item should be completed so deadlines are never missed and you stay within your marketing budget.

I suggest that you write your annual marketing calendar as a summation of your annual marketing plan. Then, put one person in charge of the plan and make sure all materials are sent out on a timely basis. Your marketing calendar will also serve as the detail needed to build your budget.

TAKE ACTION:

- Create a marketing calendar as a summation of your marketing plan.

- Dedicate one person who is responsible for marking the progress of each initiative in the plan.

CHAPTER 4

Networking Works

Networking is an important form of marketing. It's important because acquiring customers in the green industry is mostly relationship-based. One of the best ways to build relationships is by networking to meet new people. Let them know what you do and how you might help each other.

You can network with existing clients, professional contacts, friends and sports or social contacts. You can also meet people through committees you serve on and various organizations to which you belong. Basically, get to know as many people as possible and stay in touch with them.

Of course, staying in touch with people and keeping the relationship fresh is the trick. E-mail is an easy way to maintain relationships. Some companies have the time and resources to write and send out newsletters. Personal phone calls once in a while will help as well. But there is nothing like face-to-face time to build meaningful relationships. Invite your key contacts to lunch every six months or so to strenthen the relationships.

When I was in business, I joined a networking group that met every other week on Thursday mornings. Although my company did its share of residential work, we were primarily in the corporate and commercial markets. So this particular group served our needs well.

Before I joined them they had been meeting for more than 15 years. There were 15 to 20 members that regularly attended the group. Members represented a variety of businesses. There was a commercial realtor, print broker, a large national furniture mover, interior plantscaper, art broker and more. These people were great, and they really kept their eyes on our market. I always knew what companies were moving in and out of my area. I think the members of this group knew every facility manager in my entire county.

Networking is an extremely effective means of gaining new business, but as with most things, you get out of it what you put into it. As a direct result of my networking efforts, I earned the largest contract of my career and, certainly one of the largest grounds maintenance contracts in the country.

On another note, I remember vividly how I met a landscape architect in an elevator on the way to an industry meeting. I introduced myself, and after a brief discussion, he asked me if I wanted to bid on a very substantial job. Of course, I said yes. We later bid and won the job. We retained that maintenance job for more then 10 years with total billings of well over $2 million.

On another occasion, I went to a seminar about recycling. Talk about boring, but the room was filled facility managers. I saw three guys sitting at a table in the middle of the room and asked to sit with them. As soon as I did, I introduced myself and gave them my card. Turns out they all worked at a very large, well-known industrial plant, and I was sitting next to the director of facilities.

Before we parted, he gave me his card and asked if I wanted to bid on his work. Are you kidding?! You bet I wanted to. I called the next day and three months later we were doing that job. We managed this job when I sold my company, and total billing was more than $5 million.

The moral of these stories is if you are not involved in this effective marketing process, think about how you might begin. Keep business cards handy and start spreading the word.

TAKE ACTION:

- Consider joining a networking group.

- Join community organizations and network to meet new contacts.

- Stay in touch with as many decision-makers as possible.

Keep Referrals Rolling in the Door

Most companies I work with, including my former one, grow because their happy customers spread the word. They refer us to their personal and business friends. When quality work combined with good service is offered on a consistent basis, there is generally a steady stream of referrals. As a result, most companies in the green industry spend little on marketing. Two percent of sales would be a lot for most. Referrals save companies thousands of dollars each year.

As companies grow, it's especially important to remember what, or who, got them there. As I mentioned, there's no secret to earning referral business. The formula is quality work and happy customers who spread the word about your services.

Armed with this information, we should guard against even a hint of complacency because every single customer is important to your reputation. Every employee who deals with a customer either on the phone or in person should make sure that client is not just happy, but totally satisfied. You want customers to be raving fans of your company.

To make sure that referrals keep streaming in the door, be sure to reward the person who referred you. I learned the importance of reward when my little dog, Popcorn, was a puppy. Popcorn is a West Highland Terrier, more commonly known as a Westy. These dogs are cute little white puff balls when they're puppies. We just love our little guy. Anyway, I would teach Popcorn to roll over and when he did I gave him a treat. Guess what? When I asked him to do it again, he did. If I kept asking him but stopped the treats, after a while he would lose interest. Is this a simplistic example? Of course. But nonetheless, Popcorn is an awful lot like your customers in some ways.

Every single time someone tells you they were referred to your company, be sure to find out who recommended your services. Then, reward this individual.

How? Call them and thank them. Send them a handwritten note. If you get a good job, send the person who gave the referral a gift, such as flowers, a restaurant gift certificate, a great box of candy or a discount coupon for the local nursery. There are many ways to say thank you. The important thing is to show them in a memorable way that you really appreciated the referral.

If you reward customers who refer your business to others, they will tell even more people about you. Word travels. But if you don't reward them, well, like Popcorn, they will lose interest.

You can gain a lot of new customers with little effort. Then you can charge more for your services than the competition because you are in high demand.

TAKE ACTION:

- Keep in touch with all past customers.

- Make sure every customer is totally satisfied.

- Reward those who give referrals.

CHAPTER 6

Are Your Business Cards in Your Pocket?

The first type of advertising most new business owners invest in is business cards. You can create them on your home computer or you can go to your favorite local print shop. When you get your first cards, you are so proud of them that you liberally pass them out. But many new cardholders make some basic mistakes that I don't want you to make.

I gave a talk some time ago to 300 landscape business owners. I asked them who had business cards. As expected, they all raised their hands. Then I asked if they could show me their cards. It looked like only two-thirds or less of the audience had their cards with them.

Next, in a random sampling of the cards, I pointed out that many were incomplete. On some the mailing address was missing, on others e-mail addresses were omitted and some cards made no mention of a Web site the owner had invested thousands of dollars to create. The one card that was the most outrageous was one that read, "Jones Services." (I am not using the company's real name to protect the guilty.) The card contained a phone number, but no address and no mention of the services. These mistakes are all too common.

Stop reading for a moment and take out your business card. Does it have your business name, your name and position, mailing address, e-mail address, Web site, contact phone numbers and a simple statement of what you do?

Now that you have all the correct information, ask yourself while looking at your card if it matches your brand. I mean is the color and print type the same as your stationary, truck colors and other marketing materials? If not, it's time for reprinting.

Another question to ask while looking at the card is whether it is readable. A friend of mine works for a $100-million landscape company, and it is next to impossible to read his business card. The print is too light and too small. There are many companies guilty of this same problem. Some of these companies even have their own in-house marketing departments. For the life of me, I can't understand why they have business cards that are so difficult to read.

To conclude, put cards where

you keep your keys or wallet, and check to make sure you always have plenty of them with you. I recently had work done at my home and three out of five contractors did not have business cards with them. No sense in having business cards if you don't carry them. Also, print business cards for everyone at your company who has contact with customers. Your people will feel good about the cards, and customers will have all the information they need to reach your company.

TAKE ACTION:

- List all contact information and what you do on your card.

- When you meet potential customers, immediately offer them your business card.

- Check each day to be sure you have an ample supply of cards, and be sure to always take them with you. You don't want to run out.

CHAPTER 7

First Sell to Your Customers

One of the greatest sins that owners commit is not taking care of existing customers. Most of us put all of our effort into trying to get new clients, but we don't take care of the ones who have been loyal to us for years. Or, if you are a design/build company, perhaps you do not keep in touch with customers you have worked for in years past. These former customers are great resources if they were happy with your work.

I am suggesting that you visit all of the properties you maintain at least once, if not twice, a year for one purpose only. Consider how the property can be improved. Even if the customers don't purchase additional services, they will feel you are proactive and care. Because of this they will remember you and refer you to others when the subject of landscaping arises.

I know this may be hard to believe, but some residential companies make as much money doing extra work for existing customers as they do from base contracts. That can mean $1 million in base contracts and $1 million for extra work above these contracts.

How? By staying in touch with customers and suggesting ways they can improve their properties.

If you're a design/build company, you should keep all of the customers you have ever worked for in a database and keep in touch with them. E-mail or send letters to them announcing new services, new hires at your company, and your ideas for their properties. Tell them what the weather predictions are for the next six months and how this will affect the environment. Don't let them forget you.

Acquiring customers is not easy, so once you have them, treasure them and keep in touch with them. Then they will be customers for life.

TAKE ACTION:

- Inspect your customers' properties and generate ideas for improvement.

- Keep in touch with all customers you have worked for in the past so they don't forget you.

- Aim to make every client a customer for life.

CHAPTER 8

Cold Calling, A Chilling Prospect?

Cold calling is a chilling prospect for most people, but I secured millions of dollars worth of corporate, commercial and industrial work this way.

You can, too. The fear of rejection and speaking to someone you don't know is too much for some people to handle. And we all tend to avoid those tasks that do not come naturally to us.

Thankfully, if you understand the techniques of cold calling, you will overcome your fear.

When I started this type of sales, I wasn't afraid to make the calls, I just didn't know what to say. Then I came across a course on tape. I listened to the five-hour course twice, took notes and prepared myself mentally for the cold calling challenge.

The direction from the instructor on the tapes said the ideal time to make cold calls to facility managers is late Tuesday morning, Thursday afternoon and after 5 p.m. on Fridays. During the winter, I spent time compiling my "hit list" of facilities I wanted to add to our company's customer list. There were more than 200 on my list. In some cases, I found the names of facility managers and in others I eventually found who to speak with about landscaping by digging for information. I asked the person who answered the phone, and I was persistent.

In a few months, I compiled a list of corporate, industrial and commercial properties. I set aside one hour on Tuesday morning, one hour on Thursday and one hour from 5 to 6 p.m. on Friday. I made cold calls during these times for just a few weeks, and you won't believe what happened as a result of my hard work.

One of the calls I made was to a large insurance company in Stamford, Conn. I went from the receptionist to the assistant facility manager, who said, "You called just in time. We were getting ready to mail out requests for bids in the next few days."

This call led to a proposal, which led to my company winning the contract. But wait, it gets even better.

Another call I made was to a Fortune 100 company in Danbury, Conn. During the first call, I spoke to the facility manager who asked me if I could plow snow at his site. I asked him how large the parking lot was and after a brief description, I knew it wasn't large enough for me to travel the two-hour roundtrip. He understood. Then, I explained that I would send him information about my company so if something larger came up he could call us.

Almost one year later, he called me back and asked for a quote on a new facility he was going to manage. When he told me which building it was, I had to catch my breath. I made arrangements to see him immediately, and the rest, as they say, was history. This large facility paid us millions and millions of dollars during the time we maintained it all thanks to a three-minute cold call.

Make a list of accounts you would like and go after them. Cold calls are valuable for commercial and residential work. I have gone door to door in affluent residential neighborhoods and won a number of jobs I would never have gotten any other way. So make those calls. Get those jobs and grow your business. Fulfill your dreams.

TAKE ACTION:

- Educate yourself in how to make cold calls. Consider taking a class.

- Make a list of accounts you want to secure and systematically call them.

- Keep accurate records of results from each cold call.

- Do it. Make the calls!

CHAPTER 9

Trust Me – Great Proposals Build Trust

Great proposals pre-sell the jobs you're after and build the trust of your potential client. Quality proposals substantially increase your "hit rate." Yet despite these facts, most contractors pay little attention to the impression their proposals give prospective customers.

In commercial work your proposal represents you, the company, because in many cases deals are finalized before you even meet the decision-maker. Lawn care companies throughout the country measure lawns, perform assessments and put proposals on doors of potential customers without meeting them. The same is true with residential design/ build and maintenance companies. After an initial meeting, a proposal is mailed or hand delivered.

In all three types of companies, prospective customers take these proposals and compare them with your competitors. In most cases, you will not have had the opportunity to build a relationship with your prospect, so the proposal you give them is extremely important. They will judge you solely on the content in the proposal you leave them.

If your proposal looks like everyone else's, how will the prospect differentiate you from your competition? In my last two houses, one in Connecticut and the other in Virginia, I received proposals from various tradespeople. I gathered proposals from electricians, plumbers, carpenters, painters, handyman and landscape contractors. Judging from the proposals themselves, I was astounded that these contractors had any work. In the worst case, prices were presented to me on the backs of business cards; most were handwritten on preprinted proposal forms, folded up and stuffed into envelopes.

Take a careful look at what you present your prospective customer. What impression will they have when they open it? Let me offer some suggestions. First, have pre-printed presentation folders made with your company name and logo on the outside. Make sure the color of the folder matches your company colors. When the folder is opened, there should be two folds on the bottom to allow sheets to be placed in either pocket. On the outside of one of these flaps, there should be a place to insert your business card. This method gives you flexibility in what you give the customer and creates a first-class impression. If the proposal is in an envelope, make sure it is high-quality and includes your logo. The script, paper and envelope should reflect your brand.

Inside, the first thing prospects should find is a letter thanking them for the opportunity to bid on their work. Type or handwrite this on company letterhead. Next, include a sheet that explains your company history (how you started, your story), along with an insurance certificate (just a sample). Give the prospect information about you and/or your employees' education (a resume), as well as certifications, awards, state or federal licenses, pictures of other jobs, references they can contact and, finally, job specifications and the price for their job. I am fairly confident that this will be a far cry from the proposals your competition will leave.

Now that you are presenting a proposal that totally blows away the competition, please don't mail it. Call and make an appointment so you can hand deliver it. When you deliver a proposal in person, you can ask for a few minutes of the prospect's time to review it. This way, you can judge their reaction, answer any questions and close the sale, if possible.

At the end of the visit, if the prospect tells you he or she wants time to "think it over," ask if you can call them in a few days. Then mark this on your calendar and call as promised.

One of my good friends built a substantial service business in a very short period of time, so I asked him what the secret was. He said, "No secret, I just follow up a few days after delivering the proposal and no one else does. I make sure they know I want their work and I get it." This has been my experience as well.

Contractors spend their precious time visiting clients, preparing proposals and revisiting prospects, yet they don't call back and ask for the job.

Make this practice a habit and see the difference it will make. Most important, give potential customers a proposal you are proud of. If you are confident and price jobs competitively, you will win more contracts than your competitors and at higher prices. Isn't that our goal? At the same time, by writing great and accurate proposals, you build trust with customers.

Closing sales is all about trust. Great proposals elicit trust because of the great information you provide prospective customers.

TAKE ACTION:

- Deliver quality, high-class proposal packages that represent your company in a professional way.

- Try to hand deliver every proposal.

- Call back if no decision is made at time of delivery and make sure prospective customers know you want the job.

- Earn trust by delivering great proposals to prospects.

CHAPTER 10

Managing Your Sales Staff

Most people who start companies have the ability to sell jobs. In many cases, this is the owner's primary strength. As the company grows, the challenge is to recruit others to assist in this vital job. Owners who manage all of the selling responsibilities will have a difficult time handing over the reigns to others because they understand that sales are the lifeblood of the company.

Great salespeople are a different breed, and finding stable and dependable ones is not an easy task. In my experience, most are usually a bit unruly as far as the organization is concerned. While most salespeople get along well with most everyone, they don't like rules or any type of regimen. Many appear lazy because they spend a lot of time talking and doing things that appear to everyone else as unproductive, leaving reports, proposals, bids, and contracts for the last minute. Because of their personalities, you should provide salespeople ongoing time-management training.

Now that some of the negative stuff is out of the way, I have to say I love salespeople. Despite some of their common faults, they are fun

to be with, and they can do the one thing most others can't or don't like to do: sell. Great salespeople are invaluable because they drive the organization. They can meet with potential customers and return with contracts. And after a job starts, good salespeople will "upsell" and add extras or change orders, sometimes doubling or even tripling the size of the original contract. You gotta love 'em.

The best salesperson I ever had stacked papers high on his desk. There was clutter everywhere. He had the messiest office and truck. He was always the last to turn in his paperwork, especially billing. But, he could outsell everyone else in the company, sometimes even beating their combined sales.

At one point, his office was getting out of hand and after many warnings, I got so mad that I put his belongings in a large box and left it on the floor. His office was nice and clean. He was angry Monday morning, but he knew he deserved it. This forced him to clean. We still laugh about that incident today.

As owners or managers, the best thing we can do is understand the different personalities of the people we work with. Some companies assign an assistant to help do paperwork if the salesperson lags at turning in these materials. Other owners give salespeople tools like laptops to make it easier and faster for them to finish paperwork. Do whatever it takes to help them bring in those sales.

Despite the incredible value of salespeople to an organization, many owners neglect them. Those they report to don't manage salespeople properly; they don't know how to manage them at all. Salespeople are hired and let loose. They are not understood. They are judged only by their results, which is total sales per week, month or season.

But salespeople, like others in an organization, need help and regular communication from management.

One way to optimize salespeoples' results is to agree on short- and long-term goals. The goals should not just be just sales-driven. Define how many cold calls you expect per month, how many proposals salespeople must generate, how many past customers they should visit or call, etc. Then, at a minimum, hold a short meeting with your sales staff once a week.

Now you may ask, but how do we manage them? One way is with a weekly call plan. Ask salespeople to give this to you at the beginning of each week. It is, as described, a plan

of their calls and activities for the coming week.

In your weekly meeting, use the call plan as the basis for review of last week's activities. Then review the coming week. The call plan should include prospects they will meet, proposals to complete and contracts to deliver. And don't forget one of the most important things: offer congratulations for sold contracts. All of us need recognition and when a salesperson wins a big job, thank him or her. This stroking goes a long way.

An important part of the sales management process is to measure results. I learned this from a car dealer friend who maintained a large wall chart behind his desk where he tracked everyone's sales results. Now that is peer pressure. It's a good idea to post a chart on the wall in your salespeoples' offices. The chart should monitor the goals you decide on. Ask your salespeople to update the chart before each meeting. Monitoring results this way will create positive pressure and ensure that there will be no surprises.

By implementing the methods described above, you will find success in managing your salespeople. But one warning: Don't micromanage your salespeople. Agree on goals and hold weekly meetings to measure results. Then get out of their way and watch them sell.

TAKE ACTION:

- Set goals with your salespeople.

- Create and use a call plan.

- Meet weekly to review the call plan.

- Monitor results with a wall chart.

- Don't micromanage your sales team. Manage by results.

- Recognize your sales staff for their accomplishments. Feed their egos so they maintain confidence.

CHAPTER 11

How Do You Pay Your Sales People?

Since acquiring customers has a lot to do with the way you pay salespeople, it is best to include a chapter on the subject. How to pay salespeople is an age-old question and often debated. If I asked 100 companies, they would all have a different "comp" package. But before I begin to answer this question, I first need to clarify that most landscape companies don't have exclusive salespeople. If you have account managers who wear two or more hats, you are in the majority.

Most companies give these folks a small bonus or incentive for the sales they bring in. I used to give my account managers 2 percent for any new accounts. If I had it to do over again, I would probably give them 2 percent for new accounts and 3 percent for additional work they sell to existing accounts. The reason for the higher amount for extra work sales is simple. Profit margins are higher on extra work. That said, I am assuming that gross margins are being met on these jobs, otherwise I wouldn't pay anything to the losers.

Now before we go on, please don't use the percentages I cited, because every situation and company is different. The percentages you use must take into consideration the salesperson's base salary and benefits.

If you have dedicated salespeople, and I am including those who design and sell in this group, then there are three basic combinations of sales compensations. Each company probably modifies one of these three compensation methods, so you can imagine how many variations there are. Enough to fill a book! The purpose here is to cover the basics so you can take the information and apply it to your situation. Here they are:

1. Base salary no commission.
2. Commission only.
3. Base salary with commission.

Let's start with No. 1, base salary no commission.

Salaried people are generally "company" people who are happy and less stressed. They are usually quality minded and in for the long haul if they are content with their salaries. The downside is that salary doesn't always motivate a salesperson. Eventually, the person becomes a nine-tofiver. The result is stagnant sales.

Now, let's tackle No. 2, commission only.

On the pro side, commission only is great for the company because there is very little risk if salespeople don't sell. However, commission-only salespeople are interested in one thing – making sales. They are very focused on their jobs, but the caveat is that this type of salesperson could become ruthless in their attempts to win every contract. Not that every salesperson is like this, but for the most part, you'd better get out of their way.

Finally, No. 3, base salary plus commission.

By far, this is the most popular method because it offers the best of both worlds – the stability of a weekly income plus an incentive to work harder. How much salary to pay is always the question, and each company has to figure that out for themselves. It might take trial and error to achieve the right balance.

When I help clients set up sales compensation programs, I always suggest the salary plus commission method. If the salesperson is new to the company, then you may consider a much higher base, but decrease this base over time. This will allow salespeople to adjust to the new job before they must rely more heavily on commission for their pay. It may take salespeople a full year or more to get up to speed.

One mistake I have seen made, even with this method of compensation, is when companies base commission only on top-line sales without considering the profitability of jobs. This is especially dangerous if salespeople price their own jobs! Some clients have had their salespeople cheat on estimates just to sell jobs. One suggestion is to check the profitability of each job. If the job does not fall within a certain gross margin range, reduce or eliminate the commission. There are many variations to this, but the idea is to limit negative conduct and still be fair.

Yes, there are a number of factors to consider regarding salespeople's compensation. The key is to drive the behavior you want, and be fair and reasonable with your plan.

TAKE ACTION:

- Your compensation plan should drive the behavior you want from your sales people.

- Select the best sales compensation model for your firm.

- Put the plan in writing and don't forget to include the time periods you will offer commission, salary, etc.

- Pay commission for top-line sales only if you price the jobs yourself and you have job-costing systems in place to ensure profitability.

CHAPTER 12

Put Your Logos on Everything

In my travels throughout the country, I am always amazed at the number of contractors driving brand-new, shiny trucks with no lettering, logos, numbers, names, nothing! What's that about?

Contractors spend $40,000 to $45,000 on their trucks and they don't use them to advertise their companies. Trucks with company names, logos, phone numbers and Web sites are the best source of advertising there is, and it doesn't cost much. A one-time fee of a few hundred dollars will last the life of the truck. I can't tell you how many people called our office because they said they saw our trucks on their street.

Make it a policy not to drive a new truck until you put your company name and logo on it. Go to a graphic designer and make sure that what you are putting on your trucks is consistent with all your other marketing materials. (A designer will also make sure your logo is eye-catching and in good taste.)

This rule applies to larger pieces of equipment as well. Names and logos can be put on backhoes, loaders, chippers, bark blowers, anything large enough to hold your company name.

So take another look at your vehicles and equipment. Take advantage of these "moving billboards" and use them to advertise your brand everywhere you go.

TAKE ACTION:

- Put logos and names on all vehicles and equipment.

- Make it a policy that no equipment or truck "moves" until it contains your logo.

- Be sure the logos on vehicles match your brand, are eye-catching, tasteful, and easy to read.

CHAPTER 13

Direct Mail Works

A proven and successful method for obtaining residential customers is direct mail. I would only use this method for residential work. If executed correctly, direct mail will give you results; it is one of the best ways to obtain new customers in a given market area.

Direct mail marketing is generally quite cost effective. In my experience, I have found that for every $5,000 spent on direct mail, I generate at least $100,000 of new work. If this new work is maintenance, then there is no marketing cost for subsequent years. That's excellent in my opinion.

The most effective direct marketing pieces are oversized postcards. I like these because there is nothing to open, and even if people throw them away they look at both sides and get your message. Of course, originality is one of the keys to success in direct marketing, so hire a graphic designer who can produce original material. You may include great pictures of your work, or you can include cool, eye-catching artwork. In no instance do I suggest purchasing generic fliers. Keep direct mail pieces clean and simple, and don't say too much. They

say a picture is worth 1,000 words. Please, don't try to fit 1,000 words on a postcard.

The other key to success is repetition. Target the exact neighborhoods you want to work in and send one card a month for several consecutive months to the same people. I wouldn't send the same card each month; maybe the same message but change the picture. Alternate the cards. If you are not using pictures, change the message but keep the same feel. Remember, the cards should represent your brand. If you can't afford to send out at least two rounds, don't start your direct mail campaign until you can.

My consulting clients have kept track of calls received after each round of cards are sent out, and all report that after the second round, the phone rings. Timing is important. Be sure to send the cards out before and during the time you need work.

The other good thing about direct mail advertising is you can change the message depending on what type of work you are looking for. If you want to build up your maintenance department, send a group of cards featuring that service. Then you can change the message to feature your enhancements department. Again, the important thing is to establish a common theme for your cards.

TAKE ACTION:

- Target the areas where you want to gain more clients.

- Contact a talented graphic designer so your direct mail pieces are original.

- Keep cards clean and uncluttered, and use simple language.

- Send the cards before and during the season.

- Change the cards depending on the work you are seeking.

- Keep track of calls to monitor you success.

CHAPTER 14

Telemarketing

Telemarketing for residential sales is still a common practice to earn business. I personally do not subscribe to this type of marketing, and I do not recommend it to my clients. There are some large lawn care companies that successfully use this method and generate lots of leads. Many times, these companies use this annoying technique so they can generate a large volume of leads to offset a high turnover rate. Some of these companies lose up to 40 percent of their customers each year because of poor quality and/or lack of customer service. I believe there are other much more effective methods of attracting customers than this.

TAKE ACTION:

- Determine if telemarketing makes sense in your market. If it does, be the best. Otherwise, consider other types of marketing found in this section.

CHAPTER 15

Newspaper & Magazine Ads

I believe that advertisements in newspapers and magazines have value and can bring in considerable business, but much depends on the ad and frequency. In local small-town or regional newspapers, well-written and unique ads can bring very good results. The operative word is "unique." Your ad must be different. I offer the same advice with the Yellow Pages ads: Don't let newspaper or magazine people design your ad, because it will look the same as the others. Find a creative graphic designer to produce something that stands out.

One great ad that got incredible results in a local magazine was a picture of a helicopter picking up a 30-foot tree. The picture came from a job we did in 1987 for the General Electric World Headquarters Facility in Fairfield, Conn. We placed 36 30-foot trees in three atria by helicopter. For this occasion, I hired a professional photographer to capture the moment. We later turned this picture into an ad that read, "We go to any height to satisfy our customers." From this one ad, I can directly attribute more than $5 million in sales over the following 10 years.

Another example of a unique ad is one my client from a small town in Massachusetts ran in his local newspaper. His family had lived in this town for 13 generations. I suggested that we purchase a large ad and run a picture of a tree with exposed roots. In the ad, we used the tree to illustrate how his family was "deeply rooted" in the town. I wanted the ad to broadcast the idea that you could trust his family landscaping business.

Not only did we use the tree, but we included pictures of his children. A caption read that his business was supporting the up-and-coming 14th generation in the town. Corny? Absolutely. Did it work? Absolutely! He was the talk of the town, and his sales dramatically increased that year.

Another client created an ad that produced outstanding results. The ad read, "Job of the Week." He purchased space for the entire season, and each week he changed the picture in the ad. Simple, and it worked. He got calls each week that turned into jobs because of these ads. Customers and potential customers told him they looked forward to seeing the pictures each week, and that's why they called his company.

As I mentioned earlier, the key to a successful advertisement is to be unique, but I can't say enough about repetition. I vividly remember an ad in our local newspaper for topsoil. It was about 1 1/2 inch square, with the words, "Topsoil, call..." and it then gave the phone number. It ran in the Sunday newspaper for years. Did it work? Well, I certainly called when I needed topsoil.

In conclusion, consider various types of advertising in your marketing efforts. Newspapers and magazines are certainly worth a try. Be creative and have fun.

TAKE ACTION:

- Make each ad different, and change the picture or message on a regular basis to keep the ad fresh.

- Use a creative graphic designer.

- Repetition is the key. Run the ads several times.

- Track the success of the ads.

CHAPTER 16

Yellow Page Ads

The first thing most new companies do (including mine when I started out) is place a big ad in their local Yellow Pages. Is this a good thing? Well, maybe. Most of us are forced to do this because we don't know any other way. The problem is, Yellow Pages ads are expensive, and for the most part not very effective for landscape companies.

Some companies swear by the Yellow Pages, but I think most swear at them instead. I worked with a small residential landscape company in the Midwest that placed a large Yellow Pages ad for years. I have to tell you though, it was quite unique and brought them a bunch of customers each year. Running a Yellow Pages ad is a decision each owner must make for him or herself.

If you decide you want to try this form of advertising, my advice is not to let the phone company design the ad. If you do, it will look like all the others. Take your ideas to a graphic designer and challenge him or her to create a unique ad.

One warning with Yellow Pages ads: Most people who call from these ads are tire kickers. By that I mean they just want prices; the cheaper the better. Do the best you can to screen the callers so you don't waste your time going on visits to people who are not really your customers.

Finally, track in a log book how every potential customer got your name or why they are calling your company. At the end of the season, if the Yellow Pages were unproductive, you will know what to do.

These days, the Yellow Pages are being replaced by the Internet. I would rather spend my marketing money on a great Web site.

TAKE ACTION:

- If you experiment with the Yellow Pages, hire a graphic designer to create your ad.

- Screen incoming calls so you don't go on unproductive prospect visits.

- In a log book, track all potential customers so you can find out what marketing methods work.

Advertising Materials

As your company grows, you should gradually develop materials you can use for advertising and promoting your company. Some ideas might include 8½- by 11-inch pictures of your work to include in proposals or tri-folds that describe your work. You may also use these pictures for direct mail pieces and press releases. Hold on to those letters you receive from happy customers!

For small companies, creating and compiling these materials is the last thing on the owner's mind, but it is important. Set a goal to create at least one new marketing material each year. For example, take before and after photos of your work and choose the three best images. Have these englarged into letter-sized sheets to include as drop-ins for your proposals. Another goal is to create business tri-folds. These are simple brochures that you or your salespeople can give out to prospective customers. When I had my landscape business, we mailed them out, used them during sales calls and kept them in the glove compartment of every truck. Many times, interested people would stop our crew supervisors on jobs and ask for information about our company. Our supervisors gave people these tri-folds so they would know how to find us and what services we offered.

TAKE ACTION:

- Create one advertising piece each year.

- Take before and after pictures of all jobs.

- Keep brochures in your trucks for prospective customers.

Do You Need a Web Site?

As mentioned earlier, Web sites have replaced Yellow Pages in many cases. With Internet users increasing at the astounding rate of some 50,000 users per day worldwide, any business not on the Internet is really missing out. So if you don't have a Web site, it's time to invest in one pronto. Even if your business is small or brand new, a site will give you a corporate presence and build your credibility.

To begin, all you need is a Web designer and Web hosting company. Costs range from a few hundred dollars to thousands if you want a professional site. This is worth the investment. Having a Web presence is affordable and it levels the playing field. If your site is designed well, you can compete with the "big boys."

Today, most people check the Web before making any major purchases. If potential customers search online and don't find your name, you're out of luck. Even if your company was referred to someone by word of mouth, the prospective customer will look you up online before calling. On the flip side, if someone calls to inquire about services, you can refer him or her to your Web site to learn more about your company. Web sites are great information and research tools.

Whether you are contemplating creating a Web site or have one already, you want to create a crisp home page. It should be clean and uncluttered. Ask yourself these questions: Can it be easily viewed? Does it include your company contact information? Can you print out pages? Does it look and feel like your brand? Can you navigate the site easily?

These are all important questions. For example, if the home page is too busy or the print is too small, people may click right out of your site. Then you've lost them. If your site doesn't include your address, then people won't know your location. That's important if they are looking for a local person to do their work. If people can't print out pages, your company may not be considered when the husband and wife sit down to review potential contractors. And if it is difficult to navigate the site, people will become frustrated. These are all good reasons to deal with a professional Web designer, and it wouldn't hurt if they have a bit of marketing experience as well.

So to answer the question, "Do you need a Web site?" I emphatically respond, "You better have a Web site." And the more professional, the better. Get moving. I'll be looking for you "on the Web."

TAKE ACTION:

- If you don't have a Web site, it's time to create one.

- Hire a professional designer.

- Review the questions in this chapter to ensure the site is quality.

- Advertise the site everywhere possible.

PART 6

Retaining Your Customers

Chapter   1   Trust Is Everything   213

Chapter   2   Communications & Promises   215

Chapter   3   Customer Relations Management   217

Chapter   4   Customer Satisfaction & Surveys   221

Chapter   5   Managing Expectations   223

Chapter   6   Needs Assessment   225

Chapter   7   The Contract Renewal Process   227

Chapter   8   Evaluate Your Customers   231

Chapter   9   Terminate My Customers?   233

Chapter 10   Lost Job Analysis   235

Chapter 11   Romance Your Customers   237

CHAPTER 1

Trust Is Everything

People do business with people they like and trust. Where there is good chemistry, trust develops. Trust is mostly built on a series of successful, shared experiences. It was Jesus who said that he who is faithful in what is least, is also faithful in what is great. If a person can't be faithful or keep their promises in small things, how can they be trusted to fulfill large promises?

A good example of the small things is being on time for meetings or honoring commitments. Someone who places importance on the small things will be five minutes early to a meeting rather than late. When they say they will deliver a proposal on a designated date, they do it without excuses. The same holds true for job completion times and other professional commitments.

Some time ago, I had lunch with my long-time friend Pat, a contractor and entrepreneur for more than 35 years. The subject of what makes a person successful came up. He said if contractors just kept their promises and did decent work, they would be extremely successful. But most don't do that. Most contractors don't return calls as promised, they are late or don't keep appointments, they don't have proposals ready when promised and job completion dates are a joke.

People have grown so complacent. Just this week while waiting for my appointment at the dentist's office, I noticed the office manager calling to remind everyone of upcoming appointments. She said despite an appointment card given to each patient, a postcard sent out more than a week in advance and a phone call two days before, many people just "blow us off and don't even call."

This type of conduct has permeated our society today, giving those who keep their promises a huge opportunity to stand out. So build trust by keeping your promises. Stick by your word. It's not easy, but it's a worthy goal, and one that every person in your company should strive for every day with every customer. If you do business with people who become your friends and they trust you, the result is a loyal client base. Consciously building trust and friendships with your customers will give you great satisfaction. Your business will flourish and profits will flow.

TAKE ACTION:

- Don't make promises you can't keep.

- Be faithful to every promise and commitment.

- Work to build trust with every customer.

CHAPTER 2

Communications & Promises

Trust and friendships are built on experiences and communication. Have you ever had a best friend move away? If years pass without good communication between friends, a new "best friend" often takes the person's place. It's just human nature.

Communication is also essential in business, especially if you want great customer satisfaction. On the initial call, find out how your new customer wants to communicate. These days, many prefer e-mail. Others would rather talk on the phone, and some like to meet and discuss things one-on-one. Whatever your customers' preference, do it their way.

Sometimes design/build companies take weeks to complete the initial planning, designing and permitting of a job. In these situations, I strongly suggest communicating at least weekly with customers to let them know exactly what is happening. Don't let them wonder as that can lead to worry and they may begin to lose trust in you. Great contracts are often lost because of poor communication during the beginning phases of a project. Instead of growing closer to the con-tractor and sharing the excitement of the creative process, doubt and anxiety build. The client loses the enthusiasm they once had, and may hesitate to use the company for construction, or any phase of the job.

The same principle applies to on-going grounds maintenance for commercial or residential accounts. If there is no communication, the customer thinks the contractor does not care about them. So set up a schedule to contact every customer at least monthly. The important thing is that your communication shows the customer that you care.

One particular problem most contractors confront is making promises. We've talked about this before. Don't make promises you can't keep! If you break promises when you start a job, the customer will not trust you. (Please refer to the chapter on trust.) Problems that can hinder a job include weather, equipment, labor, unreliable subcontractors and materials delays. Many of these variables are beyond your control. So, be careful about making promises you might not be able to keep. It is smarter to under-promise and over-deliver. If a customer tries to pin you down to an exact date when you will start a patio, for example, tell them, "Between Wednesday and Friday." Don't say, "Tuesday at 2 p.m." Giving general time frames allows wiggle room in case problems come up. Remember to have a constant flow of communication starting at the beginning of the project. Keep talking as the project progresses, and always follow up after you finish jobs. Your customers will be impressed, rave about your company and send you referral business.

TAKE ACTION:

- Communicate with new customers in the way they prefer.

- Constantly communicate with customers during all phases of every job.

- Keep in touch with customers after the job is complete.

- Don't make promises you can't keep.

Customer Relations Management

One thing everyone would agree on is that customers are assets only if they are happy. Customers are not happy by accident, and it takes consistent, genuine and personal service delivered with quality to keep people truly happy. Now, when your employees are happy and customers are totally satisfied, the result is a strong bond.

As a company grows larger, it is more difficult to maintain close personal relationships with customers. Fortunately, there are powerful tools and techniques that can help you keep communication strong. The secret is customer relations management, also known as CRM. What is CRM? In a broad sense, companies use CRM to manage their relationships with customers. This includes the capture, storage and analysis of customer information. There are three separate aspects of CRM: operational, collaborative and analytical. For our purposes, we are interested in the operational aspects, which is basically tracking each customer's buying history in a database. Also in this database, we will store all of the information we can gather about our customer to help in our continual "bonding" efforts.

As you might imagine, companies with millions of customers have elaborate CRM databases to keep track of all the information they gather about their customers. With this information, they personalize customers' experiences so each feels the company understands their individual likes and dislikes.

Now, you may be wondering how this applies to you, the small landscape business owner. Actually, the principles are the same. As you gather data, use it to increase the bond between you and your customers.

Let me give you a little quiz regarding the top 20 percent of your customers. Let's see how well you really know them. (This applies to commercial and residential market segments.) Here we go.

First, do you know where your customers were brought up and went to school? What sports they like, and their favorite teams? What about movies, vacations, books, favorite colors? Do they have pets; what are their names? Do they spend time outdoors working in the landscape? How do they prefer to spend their disposable income? Are they married, and do they have children? Where do they work? What are their favorite restaurants in town? Do they like to travel? The list goes on.

Can you see how powerful this type of information is? We should know as much as we can about our customers because it's important to them. Do you think you would have a problem starting a conversation with a customer if you knew half of the answers to these questions? Can you see how this information will bring you closer? It's information that friends share with each other, and aren't you trying to become friends with your customers?

Now, how should you get this information? No, you don't have to hire a private detective; you can learn the answers through casual conversation. Listen to your customers and, when appropriate, ask a few well-placed questions. Over the course of time, most people will answer these questions and share bits of their lives with you. For example, if they have children, a question about them can be a great conversation starter.

Once customers tell you this information, write it down. The best way to organize it without using a computer database is on a customer profile sheet. But believe me, the best thing you can do is purchase a computer database and use it daily. Good salespeople keep their databases open to customers' profiles when they make calls on the phone, and they update this database after they hang up.

I learned a great deal about customer profiling and networking from the noted author and speaker, Harvey McKay. He has written a number of books on how this type of customer information can lead to great relationships and sales. I suggest you Google Harvey and read one of his books on the subject.

Another major reason to document customer data is because account managers and salespeople get promoted, or leave the company. If you retain customer information in a database, the new manager or salesperson can hit the decks running.

One warning: Keep all information private and only give it to individuals who need it.

After reading this chapter, you may wonder if all or this effort is worth it. Is finding out information about people's likes and dislikes really going to generate sales? Let me give you an example of how it can pay off.

I vividly remember a conversation I had at lunch with the facility manager at The General Electric Corporation's world headquarters, in Fairfield, Conn. Our company had just been awarded the contract for the grounds maintenance at the facility. I was curious about the CEO Jack Welch, and asked the facilities manager if he could offer any insight into what Welch liked and didn't like in the landscape. He responded, "Mr. Welch is an avid golfer and his passion is grass. Green grass. He loves thick, green grass."

Armed with this knowledge, when the subject of budgets came up a few

months later, I suggested we set aside money for the renovation of the area known as the "East lawn." A considerable amount of bent grass had infiltrated the lawns, and because the east section was most visible, the manager agreed with my suggestion. We were given the green light to do this work as soon as the weather broke.

As spring approached, we waited until we knew Mr. Welch was traveling and away from the site for a few weeks. We then sprayed the entire lawn with Roundup and waited a few days. We power-sliced new seed into the lawns and fertilized heavily. The entire lawn turned brown, but only for a few days. It quickly greened up as new seed germinated.

About two months later, Mr. Welch drove by the newly cut lawns early one morning and he took notice. We had mowed the lawns the day before with reel mowers; the morning sun was at just the right angle to make the grass appear so green it almost hurt your eyes. He loved it. That very morning in the company gym, Mr. Welch commented to the facility executive how great this area looked, and he asked why. The facility executive told him the East lawn had just been renovated. Welch then said, "What about the rest of the lawns?" Ah, the magic words! We were given a purchase order to renovate the rest of the 25 acres of turf on the property. That was a big win for our company.

The moral of the story is, information is powerful. This is a new way of thinking for some. It means constantly searching for data to help understand your customers better. Why and what they buy from you will no longer be a mystery. You will gain their loyalty and trust. You can virtually eliminate customer turnover, and competitive bidding will be a formality. What does all this mean to you? Customers for life, and it doesn't get better than that.

TAKE ACTION:

- Capture customer data and put it on customer profile sheets or in a computer database.

- Apply this information to servicing your customers in a way that creates a bond. They will feel that your company delivers custom work.

- Analyze the data to determine your customers' likes and dislikes. Design proposals based on this information.

CHAPTER 4

Customer Satisfaction & Surveys

Owners have mixed feelings about using surveys to measure customer satisfaction. Some owners feel if their managers really know their customers, surveys are unnecessary. They have a point. But in most companies, account managers don't really know how customers feel about them and their service. Many customers are not candid with their account managers, and will tend to hold back their opinions unless asked by a neutral party. This is why surveys are so important.

There are a few different ways to survey your customers, other than the standard written form that most companies send out. For example, call customers and ask them questions. Record their comments. A third party can make the calls, or you can assign the task to an employee that does not have regular contact with the customer. That way, the customer will feel comfortable being honest. Many high-end car companies use this method after a purchase or service.

Another suggestion is to invite your customer to a breakfast or lunch meeting for the purpose of surveying their level of satisfaction. Customers love this. This is a great way to find out what your customer thinks, and a personal meeting sends a strong message that you really care about their opinions and want to make sure they are totally happy. I used this method with the top 20 percent of my customers with great success.

Whatever survey method you choose, be sure to take the pulse of your entire customer base once a year. This way, you will uncover any hidden customer dissatisfaction.

Creating surveys is not difficult, but the questions need to be well thought out. Think about what information you need. What would be valuable to know? If in doubt, consult with a research/survey expert. This person will probably tell you how important it is that surveys are short and easy to understand.

TAKE ACTION:

- Survey your customer base annually.

- Think about the most appropriate type of surveys for your customers.

- Be sure the questions give you the right information.

- Create surveys that are short and easy to use.

CHAPTER 5

Managing Expectations

In order to have totally satisfied customers, you must manage their expectations. By this, I mean you need to be mindful of what type of work made customers happy in the past and repeat that work. For example, if Mrs. Jones likes purple and white petunias in her planters, she should not have to call to remind you of this in the spring. The account manager should record her likes and dislikes and manage what she expects: manage her expectations.

When the job is complete, she will automatically feel special. Do you manage customer expectations at your company? What happens if your account manager leaves your company? Does the new person know what Mrs. Jones' expectations are? Do you have a system set up so this annual work is completed to her expectations regardless of who handles her account?

Many businesses recognize the importance of managing their customers' expectations. The Ritz-Carlton hotel records its customers' expectations in a guest database, which is accessible worldwide. If you like to stay in the penthouse, for example, you will not have to remind them when you make your reservation; they will know. If you like a certain wine or food, they will make sure you are offered your preferences in their restaurant. If you like to sit at a corner table, that also will be noted and they will do everything possible to fulfill your wishes. The Ritz-Carlton manages your expectations.

If you want to make your customers feel special, you must keep track of all their expectations. This will shout out loud and clear that you truly care. Your customers will be loyal, and you will retain them for life.

TAKE ACTION:

- Track your customers' preferences and automatically fulfill their wishes each year.

- Create an internal system so any manager handling the account can access information necessary to deliver customer expectations.

CHAPTER 6

Needs Assessment

Another way to demonstrate to your customers that you care, and generate extra work while you're at it, is to conduct a needs assessment. This requires walking each customer's property and determining the landscape needs; always asking yourself, "Where can the property be improved?"

There's nothing new about this concept. But how many of you actually do it? The fact is, by committing a small amount of time to review each property, you can generate thousands of dollars of additional high-margin revenue. The needs assessment will also delight your customer.

When I owned my company, our goal was to put a proposal on every customer's desk every month. This was a tall order and sometimes difficult to accomplish. Howver, we worked toward that goal, and customers appreciated our interest in their properties.

Some may surmise that our customers felt like we were pushing extra work on them, or that they were being pressured with all of our proposals. But they never felt that way. In fact, it was quite the opposite. They appreciated the ideas and suggestions. We also made it clear to our customers that this was not the intent of our monthly proposals.

Our proposals varied from large to small. Sometimes they addressed maintenance issues, and other times they focused on improvements. Occasionally, we would switch account managers because we found that a fresh pair of eyes would see things differently. If the customer liked the ideas but didn't have the money, they would budget for the project the following year. It was a win-win situation for us and our customers.

We learned that when we kept a steady stream of proposals on customers' desks, they were happy. But when the proposals stopped, they complained. They complained about anything and everything. This was a weird phenomenon. We quickly realized that the time spent creating proposals was worth it.

If you are not being proactive by providing needs assessments, I suggest you start. On a regular basis, conduct a needs assessment for each account and constantly give the customer improvements to consider.

Before we close this section, I have to share a valuable experience. I had a high-profile residential client to whom we paid extra attention. Every two weeks, I personally inspected the property. Once a month, I had a tree company perform an inspection to make sure I didn't miss anything. I generated monthly status reports and suggested areas of improvement. I never heard a word from the client for the entire year.

In the spring, I received a phone call requesting a meeting. When I walked in, I could see all my proposals spread out on his desk. The client asked me why I sent them. After I explained, he thanked me and handed me back all the proposals with the instructions, "If you think the work needs to be done, then just do it!" It just goes to show, you never know.

Perform needs assessments and keep those proposals rolling out the door. Your customers will love you for it.

TAKE ACTION:

- Conduct regular needs assessments for every customer.

- Generate proposals for maintenance or property improvements.

- Don't assign the same person on the same property. Mix it up. Everyone's eyes see things differently.

CHAPTER 7

The Contract Renewal Process

Commercial landscaping contracts are typically awarded for one to three years. It's important that the customer is delighted with your service well before the renewal date. Even if your employees have done their jobs and there has been strong customer communication throughout the contract term, your client may still be required to bid the job because of a purchasing department policy. However, if you've done your job, facility managers will genearlly do everything possible to keep you. The last thing they want is a change.

Facility managers know that every change has a learning curve. They know that changing contractors can be time consuming and frustrating until the company gets up to speed.

In most areas of the country, commercial landscape maintenance has become a commodity, so contracts are usually all about the numbers. Quality and service are a given, so the contractor with the most competitive price gets the job. This means that when it's time to renew the contract, it's a good idea to think of ways to save the manager money without detract-

ing from the property. I don't mean cut corners or cheat the customer in any way. Rather, think of ways to save the customer money without anyone noticing the difference.

Let me give you an example. A friend of mine had the opportunity to bid on the grounds maintenance contract for a prestigious hotel. He took a good long look at the property prior to the bid and determined that the current contractor was doing a really great job. So he searched for a way he might save the hotel money.

Since the property had elaborate flower beds, which were a big expense to the hotel, he zeroed in on this area. When he submitted his proposal, the manager noticed the overall price was substantially lower. Of course he was delighted to see this, but he wanted to know how this savings could be achieved without detracting from the beauty of the hotel.

My friend walked the grounds with him and showed him his ideas. The manager was impressed with his ingenuity and gave him the contract. Here's the point: The existing contractor could have done the same thing, but he didn't and he lost the maintenance contract.

Many residential contractors don't have contracts with their customers. They tell me, "We have been working for them for years and trust them. We don't need contracts." But in my opinion, they are needed. Every job should have a contract.

You don't have to get fancy with fine print. Just create a simple contract that states what services you will perform, the amount, terms of payment and consequences if payment is not made. And if you don't like the word "term" contract, call your attorney and ask about using "agreement" instead. Agreement is a much softer and safer word.

Another common mistake is not using contracts for fear of creating a "moment of truth" for customers. But without a contract, there is no decision for customers to make. This might sound fine to you; you may assume your customers will ride right into the next season. But what happens when a competitor comes knocking? What if you decide to sell your company one day? How will you present your customer list to a buyer without paperwork and written commitments from customers?

I don't know about you, but I don't think I would purchase a company without written agreements with current clients. Let me give you another idea. I had a client with hundreds of residential customers. Each January, the company would send customers all new contracts. It would take them the entire month of February to follow-up and complete this task. Seeing how time consuming it was, I suggested the owner put automatic renewal clauses in his contracts.

He asked me, "How do we handle cost increases?" My suggestion was to put a cost of living increase on the first invoice, no fanfare or big announcements, just do it. He did and it worked. Did he lose any accounts? No, and he saved hundreds of hours handling contract renewals this way.

If there are price changes, just send a separate letter indicating the amount before the season begins. That way, there are no misunderstandings.

Now, there are a few caveats to all of this. In some states, like New York, multiple-year pesticide contracts are not allowed. The state requires a separate annual contract. Check into regulations in your region before considering automatic renewal contracts. Also, check with your attorney and find out how often contracts must be re-signed to remain active.

I hope these ideas either eliminate contract renewals or make renewal time easier for your company. Most of all, I hope these ideas will provide you with assurance that your customers will continue to be loyal.

TAKE ACTION:

- Require agreements for all customers, even residential.

- Make sure your customers are totally happy before contract renewal time.

- Consider contracts with automatic renewal clauses, but first check with an attorney in your state.

CHAPTER 8

Evaluate Your Customers

In the years I have been consulting, I have never come across a company that had a formal customer evaluation process. Customers are evaluating us all the time. I think it's time to turn the tables.

There are four types of customers:

1. Loyal and profitable.
2. Loyal and not profitable.
3. Not loyal and profitable.
4. Not loyal and not profitable.

In the beginning of each year, make a list of your customers and put them into one of these four groups. Let me give you some help.

Loyal and profitable – As long as you do a good job, they aren't going anywhere. They also want a lot of additional work.

Loyal and not profitable – This group includes relatives, your first customers, friends, etc. You haven't raised their prices in 10 years, and you aren't about to now.

Not loyal and profitable – This includes Mr. Big or those big corporate or commercial accounts. You are making money, but for a dollar less, you might lose them to a competitor. Watch out.

Not loyal and not profitable – Have you ever reviewed your customer list and wondered, "Why in the world are we working here?" Yes, we all have a few of these.

Now, list the customers in each group and put the total sales volume for the last season next to each. Add up the total sales volume for each group. Are you surprised? This little exercise will really help you gain perspective on your customer base.

Now let's take the next step and grade them A through D. A is the best, D is the worst. Here are some of the criteria you can use to grade each customer.

- Sales volume
- Profitability
- Location
- Ease of doing business (aggravation factor)
- Willingness to refer to others

Armed with this information, you will have a clear idea of what action to take. The following are other areas where this information will help.

- What market segment your most profitable work comes from.
- Where to adjust your marketing program to attract the most profitable customers.
- Which customers you need to charge more for services, or drop.
- How much "charity" work you are doing for relatives, etc.
- Where your customers are located and which geographic locations are most profitable.

- How much of your customer base is not loyal, but profitable. Track this risk.

If you do this exercise each season and act on your findings, your company will have better customers. This will also help marketing efforts. You will be able to focus your attention on the most profitable customers, which should translate into much higher profits. Now, that's what it's all about.

TAKE ACTION:

- Categorize all customers into one of the four groups.

- Next, grade them A through D.

- Evaluate customers and make decisions about the future.

CHAPTER 9

Terminate My Customers?

Terminate a customer?! Yes, sometimes it is necessary. Circumstances change and sometimes customers become unreasonable and demand more than you can reasonably deliver. Maybe the job was bid too low and the customer is inflexible. You may think that you lived up to your side of the agreement, but now you feel an adjustment must be made; but the customer isn't budging.

In Chapter 8, Evaluating Customers, I mentioned that you may choose to raise prices for non-profitable customers or "fire" them. Raising prices is pretty easy, but firing them sure isn't. (Although, if the decision is made to increase prices substantially, meet with them in person and explain the details to justify the cause for the increase.)

If after careful consideration you decide to terminate a customer, I suggest a personal meeting. If that is not possible, at least make a sincere phone call. You don't want bad feelings as a result of this decision.

Also, it is important to provide the customer with solid reasons for the termination. If you can do this tactfully, they usually will understand.

Finally, offer to work with the customer to find a replacement. The worst thing you can do is leave a customer high and dry. Once the non-profitable customers are cleared out, you will be able to move your crews to profitable jobs. What a concept!

TAKE ACTION:

- If you decide to terminate a customer, meet with them in person and explain the reasons.

- If possible, help the customer find another contractor.

CHAPTER 10

Lost Job Analysis

Regardless of how well we do a job, we will lose contracts. The first time I lost a really big one, I was angry and depressed. My entire staff was angry and depressed. I decided to stay angry, but only for 36 hours. Then, I came to work and told everyone, "It's over. We did all we could, and there is nothing we can do about that contract now. So let's move on and learn from what happened."

I called a meeting and we talked about the situation for hours. You see, we began to over-perform on the contract, doing things that were not called for. We were all so proud of our work. We just loved the place and truthfully felt compelled to deliver a higher-level of quality than what the customer even wanted. When the bid went out, the competition bid right to their set of specifications, while we bid it based on the hours that had been spent in previous years. When we lost that contract, it was a real dose of reality. We learned our lesson and this never happened again.

If you lose a job, it's important to find out why. Don't just shrug it off. Dig in and find out what happened. You will learn from it. Ask the customer for a meeting. Ask if there is anything that can be done to save the contract. If not, then ask if there was anything that could have been done to prevent the situation. I lost a job once and asked for an interview with the decision-makers. Before I left, believe it or not, they gave me another opportunity.

It's important to track the amount of jobs lost during the year, both as a total number and by sales volume. This way, you know how many jobs you lost and the impact on revenue for the coming year. It makes a difference if you lose 10 jobs at $10,000, or one job at $100,000. If you lost 10 jobs, I would be worried. You'd better figure out why so it doesn't continue to happen.

The fact is, you need loyal, profitable long-term customers to really make money. For goodness sakes, try not to lose the customers in the first place. Make a big deal about every job you lose. And learn from your mistakes.

TAKE ACTION:

- When you lose a job, find out why.

- Ask the customer why he or she is making the change.

- Meet with your people and analyze how the loss might have been prevented.

- Track all lost jobs by quantity and sales volume annually. That way, you can figure out the percentage of losses compared to total sales volume.

CHAPTER 11

Romance Your Customers

I hope you know I am not implying anything erotic by the title of this chapter. What I am trying to convey is that it's important that you romance your customer in the sense of showing them you care. Show them that you have passion for your work and, when possible, help them dream about the possibilities for their homes and landscapes.

Great communication skills and incredible service lay the groundwork for romancing your customers. Deliver the best from the first time they call until after the bills are paid. Show customers the love. Show them you care by doing what you promise, and by communicating with them so they always know what is going on.

Call back when you say you will, and have the proposals completed when you promise. Always follow through on the details and, for heaven's sake, make it easy for them to do business with you. Don't give customers excuses; rather, deliver indisputable results.

Romancing your customers means that they never feel their job is a transactional experience, like a purchase from the grocery store. Give them a great experience. Make them feel important; like their job is your only job.

Surprising customers with little extras is the icing on the cake when romancing your customers. If there are problems during the job, handle them immediately. When customers seem to ask for the impossible, have a can-do, whatever-it-takes attitude about fulfilling their wishes. Remember, your goal is to make sure they are totally satisfied.

If you romance your customers like this, they will be loyal and spread the word about your company. Your business will grow, your profits will soar and you will be content knowing you did the very best you could for them.

TAKE ACTION:

- Make the decision to romance your customers. (They'll love you for it!)

- Create an action plan within your company to sustain this romance by creating methods for communicating and responding to issues.

- Make sure every customer is happy and totally satisfied so they spread the word about your business.

PART 7

You

Chapter 1   Vision   241

Chapter 2   Values & Virtues   243

Chapter 3   Remove the Road Blocks   247

Chapter 4   Delegate Everything Possible   249

Chapter 5   Learn to Manage   251

Chapter 6   People Skills Are a Must   253

Chapter 7   Attitude *Is* Everything   255

Chapter 8   Control Your Emotions   257

Chapter 9   Take Vacations   259

Chapter 10   Are You Ready to Sell?   261

Conclusion   263

Resources   265

Recommended Reading   267

CHAPTER 1

Vision

Vision comes from the top, usually from the owner. My definition of vision is simply the answer to the question: "What do you want?" What do you want out of your business? Where are you going? Vision is the big picture. Take time each year to think this through and then simply write down what you want. Vision that is not written down is just a dream, so find some quiet time and take notes. Write down your thoughts, your ideas, what you want the future of your business to look like.

The greatest story I ever heard that illustrates the power of vision is about Walt Disney. After Disneyland in California was built, Walt Disney wanted to create another, even better park somewhere else. The company conducted extensive research and found land in Florida, where Disney World is now located. While the plans for the new Disney World were under way, Walt Disney died. But construction moved forward. During the dedication of this incredible place in Orlando Florida, some said, "Too bad Walt isn't here to see this." The response was, "He already has."

Yes, Walt Disney had envisioned the entire place in his mind and helped plan much of what Disney World is today. His vision was so powerful that even after his death, the Disney people worked tirelessly to fulfill his dream, his vision.

Small business owners are so guilty of working without a vision. We work day in and day out, not knowing what we may be building or where we are headed.

You have probably heard the words of the great philosopher Yogi Berra. "If you don't know where you're going, how do you know when you get there?"

Many owners are stumped by this question. The truth is, they don't know where they are going. Their business is just a place to go to work.

Now, let me give you a classic example of the power of vision. About three years ago, I visited a small contractor who for some time had been thinking about giving up his business to accept a "solid reliable job" with a local builder. He had been working for himself for years, with total sales never exceeding $210,000. There was never quite enough left after paying expenses to properly provide for his family. He was discouraged. At the end of a day spent discussing his business, sitting at his dining room table, I told him, "I think I know what your problem is." He said, "What is it?"

I replied, "You have no vision, so I'm going to give you one. If you like it, you can keep it." He said, "What is it?" I told him confidently, "You are going to have sales of $1 million within the next five years. And, you are going to be the go-to company in your market."

He repeated, "$1 million in five years? That's it? That's the vision?" I responded, "Yes, that's it."

He silently thought about this and after a few moments, he said, "Are you going to help me?" I responded, "Absolutely. That's what I do. I help make millionaires."

At the end of that season, his sales were more than $400,000. The fol-lowing year, sales exceeded $600,000. As of this writing, he topped the $1 million goal. He did it in four years!

Oh, and one more thing. Last year, he fulfilled another part of his vision. He purchased property and now has a "home" for his business. He is fulfilling his vision, and so can you if you write it down, be specific, create a plan and work toward it every single day.

Once you have a vision of what you want, share it with your people. Make it their vision, too. If they accept and buy into the vision, they will work with you and help you fulfill it, just like the Disney people did.

So, why not take some time off from the rat race and think? Think about what you want for yourself and your business. Commit it to writing, focus on fulfilling your dream each day, and soon it will become reality.

TAKE ACTION:

- Think about what you want and create a vision.

- Write down your vision and create a plan to accomplish it.

- Share your vision with your people.

- Work toward your vision every day and it will become a reality.

CHAPTER 2

Values & Virtues

The most important part of a company's true equity is not its trucks, customer list, buildings or equipment. True company equity consists of the values and virtues of its owner, leaders, management and people. What do I mean by values? My definition is this: an unwavering set of principles and standards that are practiced each and every day. A company true to its values is a powerful thing.

Virtues are goodness; the fairness that is displayed by leaders and managers. When leaders are virtuous, they build trust. How important is trust? Trust is everything. If your people trust you, they will trust each other, and in turn, customers will trust your company and remain loyal. Companies grow because customers trust their products and people. Trust is what builds these companies' reputations. At the end of the day, it's what both your business and personal reputation is all about.

You need trust to grow your customer base, retain your people, and work with suppliers. You must trust your bank, your advisors and your management team. Trust is the glue essential for building a successful business.

Some owners steal from customers in terms of quality or quantity. Why do they do it? I don't really know. Maybe they are afraid they will not make enough money otherwise. Maybe owners "steal" out of greed or fear. Regardless of the reason, their people see it. They know what's going on. Employees that see owners stealing from customers will feel free to steal from the company. They will steal materials, equipment and even worse, time. They won't think twice about it either, because stealing is one of the "values" set by the owner or management.

However, if the owner has integrity and lives by high standards, his people will see that too. The result? Respect for the owner and the company. A company like that will grow and prosper.

In order to have the people in your company, especially new ones, clearly understand your values and what your company is all about, it's good to create a value statement. Value statements describe how people should behave with each other in your organization, as well as with your vendors and customers. Personal and cultural values are principles and qualities that guide your actions.

Think about your life. What values have been your cornerstones? Values that are formed during childhood build the foundation of our personalities, providing us with direction in life. If you think about it, your values have determined who you are and where you are going. Can you see the importance?

Why not take the time to identify in words the values that describe what is most important to you? What values are critical to ensure the success of your organization? There are usually up to a dozen words that really describe who you are.

Now, this process doesn't get done during a one-hour meeting. Values run deep and must be discussed and vetted for a period of time before you will arrive at the words that truly describe the core values of you and your company.

Some examples of values include: accomplishment, accuracy, beauty, orderliness, commitment, competence, continuous improvement, discipline, excellence, faith, family, freedom, hard working, honesty, integrity, loyalty, love, peace, perfection, punctuality, speed, success, achievement, trust, unity and wisdom.

Find a complete list of words that encompass your many values and review them with your people. Take your time. Start with a number of possible values and keep narrowing it down until you have somewhere be-

tween six and 12. Then, once you all feel this truly represents and encompasses how you and your people feel, create a value statement from that list of words.

Make the statement or group of words as concise as possible. Here are three examples.

Microsoft's values: As a company, and as individuals, we value:
- Integrity and honesty;
- Passion for customers, for our partners and for technology;
- Openness and respectfulness;
- Taking on big challenges and seeing them through;
- Constructive self-criticism, self-improvement and personal excellence;
- Accountability to customers, shareholders, partners, and employees for commitments, results and quality.

IBM's values:
- Dedication to every client's success;
- Innovation that matters, for our company and for the world;
- Trust and personal responsibility in all relationships.

General Electric's values:
- Curious
- Passionate
- Resourceful
- Accountable
- Teamwork
- Committed
- Open
- Energizing

General Electric concludes it's list with the statement, "Always with unyielding integrity."

There you have it; some excellent value statements to give you an idea of how to craft your own. Now it's time to go to work and create the words or statements that will lead your company into the future.

TAKE ACTION:

- Ask key managers to list the values that they believe represent the company.

- In subsequent meetings, narrow the list to approximately six values.

- Use these words as descriptors for your values, or create statements for each word.

- Operate your company based on your values.

CHAPTER 3

Remove the Road Blocks

There are four essential functions an owner must perform or oversee in a business: sales, production, financial management and overall operations. An owner play all four roles in the beginning, and later when the company grows, the owner will delegate responsibilities to other reliable employees. In the process, the owner must serve as coach and cheerleader to help the team maintain a positive attitude.

When I started my company, I knew I had to wear the "sales hat" among many others if I wanted my business to grow. I lived by the motto, "If it's to be, it's up to me." I didn't particularly care for the bookkeeping, accounting, general paper work, equipment maintenance and the myriad of things that have to be done in a landscape operation.

Many owners focus on the sales part; that's why they went into business. That's what they enjoy. Others love the work and don't really like to deal with the customers. Whatever your inclination, when business is jumping, all of these tasks must be done, and you're ultimately responsible for seeing them through.

We all gravitate to what we like to do, to those areas where our talents lie, to the tasks that interest us. The rest of the work is just one, big hassle. But the fact is, those hassles, usually the paperwork, are important jobs that someone must complete. As the owner, it's up to you to get it done.

In my experience, these incomplete jobs, the ones owners may avoid, can create a bottleneck that prevents growth and real success. My advice is to find someone capable of doing this work as soon as you can possibly afford it.

Owners call me all the time to complain about how they have been in business for five, 10, 15 or more years and just can't grow. They don't know why they can't make "good money." In most cases, I find this happens because of a lack of planning, or not addressing certain tasks vital to the company's operation, or not taking the next step and hiring employees to wear some of these "hats." So, owners become slaves to the business and work too hard to make a living. In reality, the owners are the roadblock to their own companies' growth and profits. They are creating the bottleneck. If this is your case and you have had enough, it's time for a change.

What to do? Perhaps it's time to take a fresh look at your business. Bring in a consultant who specializes in the green industry or has worked in the business before. This may sound a bit self-serving, but the truth is the truth. A complete review of your operations by someone from the outside will bring to light what is causing the bottleneck. Maybe you need a good operations manager, bookkeeper, administrative assistant or salesperson. I have seen many companies blossom once these positions are filled.

Or, perhaps your company is in need of systems and processes. Perhaps there are problems associated with pricing, estimating or labor efficiency that could be holding you back. Whatever the problem, don't you be the roadblock to solving them. Instead, discover what changes need to be made and take action so your company can grow and profit.

TAKE ACTION:

- Determine your strengths and weaknesses.

- Are your weaknesses holding back the company?

- Conduct a personal analysis or bring in an outside business consultant.

- Make necessary changes.

CHAPTER 4

Delegate Everything Possible

I f you've ever been to a live or-chestra performance or watched one on TV, you have seen how the conductor directs the players but does not play any of the instruments. If the conductor were to sit down and play trumpet, then the entire orchestra could get out of sync. Not a good thing for an orchestra. This happens because the players can no longer see the leader clearly, and the leader is distracted playing his own part.

If the orchestra is small, this arrangement might work for a while, but certainly at the expense of the orchestra leader. The conductor will run himself ragged trying to keep the musicians playing while he focuses on the trumpet part. I find the orchestra example to be a great metaphor to clearly understand what happens in so many small landscape companies. Owners want to play in the orchestra and be the conductor. But it's a difficult position to be in for any length of time without having "the orchestra" get off beat.

I've talked to many owners in this situation, and they usually defend their position by saying they need to be "hands-on" and "in the trench-es" because there is no one else who can do the job. When I hear this, I wonder if they have ever deliberately worked with a person on their staff or hired someone with the ability to help with the conducting. Usually, the result of this lack of delegating is limited growth and considerable pressure on the owner.

Becoming the "conductor" in your company requires growing to the point where you can afford not to have to work in the field. You must find and educate the right players. Key to this is making strategic hiring decisions based on your needs today and tomorrow.

For example, one landscape architect client told me she planned to hire a supervisor to run her crews. She needed help because she was doing everything herself and did not have time to focus on her love – the design work. My advice to her was to hire a crew supervisor with management capabilities to run all of the crews in the future. In essence, hire a person who can take over many of her responsibilities in the future. This might cost more in the short-term, but she would be much better off in the long-term. Then, as the business grows, that supervisor eventually may be in the position to manage the overall operation, freeing her to focus on design. This owner needed a "lieutenant" in place so she could grow the company.

The real lesson here is to delegate as much as possible and as soon as possible. That way, you will have the opportunity to work on the business and not just in it.

TAKE ACTION:

- Delegate as much as possible to your people so you can work on your business and not just in it.

- Hire qualified leaders who can take over managerial responsibilities so you can focus on growth.

CHAPTER 5

Learn to Manage

Good leaders need to be able to see not only the big picture, but also to focus on the little stuff. If they can't do both, they need to realize this and hire people with skills who can "shore up" their weakness.

Some owners have the ability to drill down and deal with the details, but in doing so, they sometimes lose sight of the big picture. Some obsess about the small things and forget what really matters. Others can move the company forward by obtaining huge contracts, hiring awesome people, co-coordinating operations, etc., but neglect the details that are required to maintain profitability.

A "macro/micro" balance is required to be successful. If you don't know which type of person you are, figure it out quickly so you can exploit your strengths and hire others to compensate for your weakness. Owners of successful companies know if they are macro- or micromanagers. Most people are not a perfect balance of both. If they are the type of people who love to put the deals together and make the big sales, but they hate details, they should hire detail-oriented managers. On the other hand, if they are the type who love to work through details, they should surround themselves with people who see the big picture and can drive the company forward.

A balance of both qualities – big picture and detail-oriented – is needed to have a truly successful company. Analyze yourself and the people you work with to be sure there is proper balance. As the owner, your responsibility is to ensure that your team can manage the big and small stuff.

TAKE ACTION:

- Determine whether you are a macro or micro leader.

- Hire people to cover your weaknesses.

CHAPTER 6

People Skills Are a Must

It's critical to be able to understand and motivate people and to communicate well with them. In order to do this, it is important to study the four main personality types. These are directors, socializers, analyzers and workers.

The directors lead. They make things happen. The socializers are communicators. They are the salespeople who sell your products and services, and they're generally happy-go-lucky, fun people. The analyzers are thinkers. They are the people who do the accounting and track the detail work no one else wants to do, but is so necessary. Last, but not least, are the workers, who are responsible for carrying out everyday operations. The workers are the largest group, without them nothing would happen.

It is extremely important for owners, leaders and managers to understand how each of these four groups of people work with one another. It is important to understand their strengths and weaknesses and to realize where each group fits into the company mix.

Andrew Carnegie was the world's first billionaire. He earned his fortune in the steel business. He attributed his success to the ability to hire great people for his business. He understood what made people tick.

The same is true today. Your people make your company tick. Make sure you have the right balance of personality types in your company. Can you imagine if they were all of the same personality type? Take the time to understand them and how they work. What qualities do they contribute to your company?

Without a doubt, one of the keys to success is getting along. This means an owner must motivate people, and hire the right people in the first place. There are courses on tape, seminars and books that can help you learn more about this all important area. If your people skills are weak, I urge you to take advantage of readily available information. Communication and understanding are critical to your success as an organization. By the way, which personality best describes you?

TAKE ACTION:

- Seek an understanding of each of the dominant personalities.

- Determine your dominant personality.

- Hire the right personality for each role in your company.

CHAPTER 7

Attitude Is *Everything*

Most owners don't see themselves as leaders, but they should. Like it or not, every owner has the opportunity to be a leader. Some owners do a great job in this position while others do not. But either way, leaders' attitudes profoundly impact the people who work in their companies.

Some years ago, I visited the co-owner of a landscape company with sales of slightly more than $25 million. He handled the operations of the company, and his partner managed the administrative responsibilities. I asked the owner what time he arrived at work each morning. He said "No later than 5:30 a.m." I was a bit surprised, so I asked him if he had an operations manager. He said he did, and that the manager handled all facets of his operations. That sparked my curiosity.

I asked why he was in so early, especially if his operations manager was busy preparing crews. His answer was incredible. He said he thought of himself as a coach. He greeted everyone as they came in each morning with a big "good morning" or "how ya doing?" or "how did it go yester-

day?" He added, "I ask a lot of questions, pat them on the back and figuratively kick them in the butt when they need it. The bottom line is they know I care."

Like any good coach, he listened to his workers' problems, celebrated their successes, set the pace and got everyone out in a positive frame of mind each day. Can you picture this? I think this positive energy is working. In just five years, the company will earn $40 million in sales.

No one wants to be around grumpy, negative people. If you go to work and act like you don't want to be there, then why would your people? Some owners walk around in the morning barking orders while others go to their office and shut their doors without saying good morning to anyone. These actions do not foster positive attitudes. If these scenarios sound like you in the morning, think about how your demeanor affects your people. You are figuratively killing them.

We're all human. Once in a while when I owned my landscape business I would get into a funk. When I did, I would leave the office rather than infect others with my bad mood.

Sometimes a change of pace is needed, or maybe just a good night's sleep.

On the other hand, people with positive attitudes energize others. A positive, can-do attitude fosters creativity, quality and productivity.

Keeping a positive attitude is so important.

It may be corny, but I think the words of the old song are true. "When you're smiling, when you're smiling, the whole world smiles with you."

TAKE ACTION:

• As the leader of the company maintain a positive attitude.

• Encourage and explain why a positive attitude is so important in your company.

CHAPTER 8

Control Your Emotions

As the owner, leader or manager of a company, you never want your people to see you out of control. I've heard about owners who have fits of anger. How damaging. This type of conduct can wipe out respect. People generally will not work as hard for an owner/manager they have little or no respect for. They will not be loyal to them. In contrast, owners held in high regard by their people are in control of their businesses and their lives.

Don't misunderstand me. We're all human and have emotions. We laugh, we cry and at times get angry. What I am talking about is control. Let me give you an example. When I was just out of high school, I worked in a restaurant. One day, I witnessed the owner throw a pot as hard as he could across the kitchen, some 25 feet. It rang out as it crashed against the wall. He did it because someone complained about the food. That pot could have killed anyone in its path.

Later that day, the head chef had a serious talk with the owner, explaining how his actions might have seriously injured someone. He told the owner how people in the kitchen lost respect for him because of his outburst. This was sure true of me. I was wondering if I was working for some kind of lunatic. The chef then tactfully warned the owner if such a thing happened again, he would no longer work at the restaurant. I can tell you, this warning had a profound effect on the owner and he never lost his temper again while I was working there. But I'll tell you what, I never did trust the owner again.

When I first started my business, I used to get excited and/or upset when under pressure. One day, a friend counseled me about this. He said, "When you get excited, you can't think clearly." He was right. He continued, "Have you ever noticed the great composure the presidents of the United States have when under pressure? They may be nervous or excited on the inside, but they never show it. They always appear cool, calm and collected."

I thought about what he said. I remember when John F. Kennedy was President and spoke to the American people during the Cuban Missile Crisis. This was, without a doubt, one of the most dangerous periods in our history. A very dear friend of mine was the captain of a B-29 bomber with a nuclear bomb on board. He told me when he was given the instructions to "arm the bomb," his heart pounded thinking this was going to be the end of the world. All he could think about were his wife and children below.

You can imagine that the "weight of the world" was on President Kennedy. Yet, he got on TV that evening and explained the situation. He spoke in a calm, confident yet firm manner. He reassured the American people. My parents felt better after his talk and so did I. What a great example of how the composure of one man can have such a positive effect on so many people. It's a true sign of leadership.

Another more recent example of a person keeping complete control was Rudolph Giuliani, the mayor of New York City, during the 9/11 crisis. Not once did he appear flustered. What an example he was for us all. I saw a great interview on TV. Mayor Giuliani said he could not, would not allow himself to lose control. He did say, however, that after seeing so much death and destruction, three days later he went home and wept uncontrollably for about a half hour.

Hopefully, we will never have to face such monumental pressures. But these examples really demonstrate the point. When we maintain control over our emotions, we are respected; when we don't, people lose respect for us. In business, this respect translates into confidence, which allows for success.

TAKE ACTION:

- Don't ever allow yourself to lost control of your emotions.

- Leaders keep their composure under pressure and, as a result, are respected. Follow their example.

CHAPTER 9

Take Vacations

After launching a company, many owners work 10 to 12 hours a day, six days a week for years before they can begin to work more reasonable hours. I know because this was true in my case. But once the foundation of the company is established, look for a person who can assume some of your responsibilities. If you don't find someone you can trust and begin this transition, you will get in a rut that many owners know well.

Many owners of multi-million dollar businesses still work incredibly long hours. There is no doubt that there are busy times of the year and a "do whatever it takes" attitude is necessary. But when that busy period is over, we really need to "get a life."

My former company was located in Connecticut so I lived and worked through crazy times each spring. Mike Rorie, one of my landscape friends from GroundMasters in Loveland, OH, calls spring "the 100 days of hell." I never forgot those words because they are so true. But no matter how crazy it got, I never worked on Sunday. And once those 100 days were over, I returned to a more normal life.

Before I leave this subject, I want to comment on time off and vacations. Many owners don't take vacations, or if they do they are few and far between. They believe it is impossible to get away from the business and that the business cannot run without them. Well let me tell you, that is baloney. If you use this excuse, you are making a big mistake.

You need to get away to rest your body and mind. If you can't get away from your business for at least a week, then it's time to begin to put the necessary people in place so you can. If you don't get away after a period of time, you will burn out and lose life balance. There are countless business owners who just wear out after 15 years or so working crazy hours and handling all of the pressures. Am I describing you? If so, it's time to restore balance in your life. Take a vacation.

TAKE ACTION:

- Take time off away from your business.

- If you feel you can't take time off, it's time to put people in place in your company so you can.

CHAPTER 10

Are You Ready to Sell?

I began my company in 1971. In 1980, we hit a milestone. We were awarded a large and prestigious contract – the grounds maintenance at the General Electric World Headquarters in Fairfield, Conn. This was a premier commercial account in the Tri-State New England area. With the GE contract secured, many more followed. Before we knew it, our company was simultaneously maintaining the world headquarters for 10 of the world's largest and most powerful public corporations.

In 1998 and 1999, three large companies called wanting to buy me out. I had never considered selling my company. I wrestled with the offers. After serious deliberation, I made the decision to sell. It made sense because I was receiving good offers, and I had been in business for nearly 30 years. It was time for a change.

Competition was heating up, and large national landscaping companies were coming into the area. The glamour and glitz of running and owning a company had worn thin. For a number of years prior, I had dreamed of becoming a public speaker, writer and consultant. If I sold my busi-

ness, I could work toward fulfilling my dream; my vision. I was fortunate because while I did not have an exit strategy, my hard work building a professional company paid off. I realized later why my company was so attractive to buyers. Here are a few reasons:

- I had the best accounts in the entire state.
- I had great people.
- The company could run virtually without me.
- I had a recognized and respected name/brand.

Of course, hindsight is 20/20. My inexperience resulted in me getting a lower price for my business, but I do not for one minute regret my decision to sell. Today I am living my dream. My potential is unlimited.

As of this writing, the thirst for acquisitions has slowed, buyers have become highly selective of their business targets. When I consult with owners who tell me they are thinking of selling, I tell them it's best to take six months to a year to groom their business for a sale before they even think about approaching potential buyers. Like selling a used car, the business must be washed, waxed and detailed to attract buyers.

Let me list some of the factors that attract buyers. When all of the items listed below are in place, an owner will have improved the business valuation and thus attract more desirable buyers.

1. A stable customer base.
2. Good record of profitability.
3. Well-organized financials.
4. Minimal insurance claims.
5. Great people.
6. The ability to run efficiently without the owner.
7. Written contracts with each and every customer.
8. Promising potential for future expansion.
9. Flexible payment options for your customers.
10. An owner willing to stay during the transition period.

These 10 items are a tall order and will take diligence to achieve. I feel owners need outside help to accomplish all of these tasks. Let's face it, as owners we are not always objective. We can't always clearly see our strengths and weaknesses. We all hire experts to guide us in legal matters, complete our taxes, buy and sell our homes, maintain our health, etc. Doesn't it make sense to work with professionals to prepare your business for sale?

Whether you want to sell your company now, you should always operate as if you were selling tomorrow. You never know. Think about your exit strategy and hire professionals to help make and keep the company "shiny."

TAKE ACTION:

- Run your company as if you were going to sell it tomorrow.

- Work with professionals to maximize profits and keep the operation "shiny."

CONCLUSION

Business – You Gotta Love It!

Business is exciting. Business is fun. Markets change, people change, equipment is changing and you change. Everything is changing. Some change is fast, while some is slow. Either way, all change creates excitement. Optimizing profit is challenging, and profit is how we keep score. It's what adds to the excitement.

Work with a positive attitude. Work conscientiously and with awareness every day. Keep asking why things are the way they are and how things can be done better, faster and smarter. Take time to think. Reserve time to ponder problems and opportunities with other kindred spirits.

Take the time to dream and follow those dreams. Take the time to create a plan of action to accomplish those dreams. Then, work hard and execute your plans. Follow your plan, but be sure to have fun along the way. And, be sure to celebrate your successes as they come.

Work at business seriously, but put your relationship with God, family and loved ones first, because when you look back, you don't want to have any regrets. Work hard and smart and thoroughly enjoy every day while doing it.

Owning a business is not easy. If it were, everyone would start one. Success will require many positive qualities, but an average person who is persistent can achieve incredible success. Business success is a great deal about relationships. So be deliberate, and cultivate and maintain these relationships. And lastly, be sure people respect and trust you.

I hope the practical knowledge in this book has helped you, whether you are new or a veteran in business. I wish you the best. If you need help, I am here for you.

RESOURCES

Ed Laflamme & Associates
www.edlaflamme.com
info@edlaflamme.com
voice 203-858-4696

Professional Landcare Network (PLANET)
www.LandcareNetwork.org
950 Herndon Parkway, Suite 450
Herndon, VA 20170
Voice (800) 395-2522

- *Operating Cost Study*
- *Crystal Ball Reports*
- *Pricing for the Green Industry*

RECOMMENDED READING

The E-Myth (Revisited)
by Michael Gerber

Winning
by Jack Welch

The 9 Super Simple Steps to Entrepreneurial Success
by Martin J. Grunder, Jr.

Execution
by Larry Bossidy

Your Management Sucks
by Mark Stevens

Your Marketing Sucks
by Mark Stevens

First Break All the Rules
by Markus Buckingham

Good to Great
by Jim Collins

The Great Game of Business
by Robert Stack

Open Book Management
by John Case

Pricing for the Green Industry
by Frank Ross

Think & Grow Rich
by Napoleon Hill

Flawless Execution
by James D. Murphy

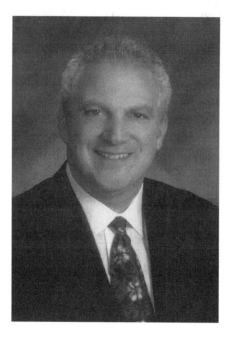